D1074352

Applause for ... *Rio* ♥ *A Love Story*

"Rio - A Love Story is a beautifully written love story indeed, a love story of a mother and her children and the special love story many of us have experienced with a beloved pet. Poignant and compelling, Joni takes the reader on a powerful journey from tragedy to triumph. The book is a testament to both the strength and resilience of the human spirit and how the unselfish love between a dog and a trainer can heal both. Highly recommended."
—*Bradley Rand Smith, Internationally Award-Winning Playwright, Screenwriter, Theater Producer and Director*

"I wasn't prepared to feel the depth of emotions I did when I read *Rio – A Love Story*. I guess I thought there wasn't a dog story I hadn't already heard. My life has been for dogs and about dogs — my own and other's — for most of my adult life — and especially since I started my own dog bakery and boutique more than 15 years ago. But as I was reading Joni's book, I realized that I was in the possession of something very special: A beautifully written love story that is at once unique to Joan and Rio, but also an acknowledgement in general of the glorious bond between dogs and their humans. I loved this book. It reminded me of how lucky I am to share space with these wonderful creatures we call our best friends."
—*Penny Milligan, Owner of the Hungry Hound, Somerville, New Jersey*

"Joan's personal and private journey as she wears her heart on her sleeve and shares her deepest life moments for all the world to see. When that one special heart dog enters her life, the insight she gains and learns from living with a blessed boy named Rio changes her very existence

with his love, devotion, loyalty and a bond that will exist for all eternity. We should all be so privileged to have that once in a lifetime soulmate dog in our lives."
—*Jennifer W. Basile, Trainer/Owner West Milford Dog Training Center, West Milford, New Jersey*

"*Rio – A Love Story* is a true love story - a love story about the type of love we all crave and all deserve - unconditional love. A must read! I read it and I loved it."
—*Tom Bird, Best-Selling Author*

"This beautiful portrayal of Joan's journey through tremendous grief, and the discovery of new meaning for life with her best friend, Rio, is well written, heartwarming and inspiring. Joan and Rio show us how having a best friend by your side, no matter what, can make the heartaches of life more bearable and the celebrations of life more amazing! Stepping out of her grief to fulfill her promise to Rio, Joan discovered the healing made possible by her willingness to love and be loved, regardless of species. As an animal communicator, I recommend *Rio - A Love Story* to you. Go home now and start listening to your dog, you just never know where that might lead you."
—*Karen Collyer, Author, Editor & Founder, Rainbow Animal Sanctuary, Tasmania, Australia*

"An emotional and heart-felt sweet journey of life's losses, adventures and new friendships. Joan's life was enriched by sharing dog sports with the renowned, remarkable and very romantic Belgian Tervuren Rio who serves loyally as her life's beacon, best friend and soulmate and redeems her life in this sweet story."
—*Lisa Pattison, KPA-CTP, CNWI, CTDI, Expert Dog Trainer, Canine Partnership, Readington, New Jersey*

"*Rio – A Love Story*, by Author Joni darc Shepherd, is a poignant story about how so many of us in this world let the everyday events in our life lead us to depression. As a dog owner myself, my little Rascal more than took me out of depression, he taught me the power of unconditional love. Rio did the same with Joan. This is a must read for anyone suffering from depression. Get a dog and your life will change for the good forever."

—*JohnEGreek, Award Winning and Amazon Best-Selling Author*

Dear Alex,
From one dog lover to another! I wish you happiness, joy and health always! Best of luck with you new dog! With love, Joni & Rio ♡

Rio ♥ A Love Story

How My Dog Saved My Life

JONI DARC SHEPHERD

Rio ♥ *A Love Story*
How My Dog Saved My Life
by Joni darc Shepherd

Published by Sojourn Publishing, Inc.

For permissions:

Joni darc Shepherd
joanandrio@gmail.com

Hardcover ISBN: 978-1-64184-151-1
Paperback (Color Edition) ISBN: 978-1-64184-152-8
Paperback (B&W Edition) ISBN: 978-1-64184-174-0
ebook ISBN: 978-1-64184-153-5

Disclaimer

I have tried to recreate events, places, and conversations from my memories of them and attempted to make this a sweet and perfectly told story. But sometimes one's memory has a mind of its own and its own story to tell. The conversations in this book may not be verbatim, though they are intended to evoke the feeling and meaning of what was said. To maintain their anonymity, in some instances I may have changed the names of individuals and places. Although the publisher and I have attempted to ensure that the information in this book was correct at press time, we do not assume, and we hereby disclaim any liability to any party for any loss, damage, or disruption caused by errors or omissions, whether such errors or omissions result from negligence, accident, or any other cause. Moreover, this book is not intended as a substitute for medical advice. The reader should consult an appropriate professional healthcare representative in matters relating to health and with respect to any symptoms that may require diagnosis or medical attention.

Dedication

I dedicate this book to my beloved Rio, who led and supported me on my journey as I rediscovered the magic of life. Rio, who is a better being than I could ever be, inspired and helped me to become who I am today, and gave me the desire to continue to become even more than I am now.

Whoever said that diamonds are a girl's best friend never had a dog or knew Rio.

And of course, I give my love and thanks to my dear family, friends and others who helped me on this incredible journey of discovery.

Contents

Introduction xv

CHAPTER 1   The Beginning 1

CHAPTER 2   The First Belgian 5

CHAPTER 3   That Belgian Magic 10

CHAPTER 4   Shaolin and Marly 14

CHAPTER 5   Nice to Meet You, Zane and Rio! 19

CHAPTER 6   Entering the Show World 23

CHAPTER 7   Let the Shows Begin!! 27

CHAPTER 8   Trials and Tribulations 34

CHAPTER 9   Pat 39

CHAPTER 10   Life After Dad 45

CHAPTER 11   System Failure 50

CHAPTER 12   It's All Down Hill 54

CHAPTER 13   Learning the Ropes 61

CHAPTER 14   Catching It All 66

CHAPTER 15 The Miracle 70

CHAPTER 16 Pat's Decline. 74

CHAPTER 17 The Storm. 79

CHAPTER 18 Learning Pains. 84

CHAPTER 19 Missing Pat. 88

CHAPTER 20 Mom and Bijou 91

CHAPTER 21 Mom's Turn 96

CHAPTER 22 Another Storm 100

CHAPTER 23 Chaos of Growing Up 105

CHAPTER 24 Let's Go Mum! 111

CHAPTER 25 The Champ. 116

CHAPTER 26 Good Citizen Meets Romeo 124

CHAPTER 27 Rally On! 129

CHAPTER 28 Run for the Door 156

CHAPTER 29 Veteran 160

CHAPTER 30 Meet the Breeds 167

CHAPTER 31 National to Westminster 171

CHAPTER 32 Are You Obedient? 175

CHAPTER 33 I Herd You!. 182

CHAPTER 34 Farm Dog! 189

CHAPTER 35 Boy, Girl, and Dog Scouts 192

CHAPTER 36 Temperament and Rats 195

CONTENTS

CHAPTER 37   The Nose Knows 202

CHAPTER 38   Agility. 207

CHAPTER 39   Trick or Treat and Other Fun
             Sports 211

CHAPTER 40   Shall We Dance? 216

CHAPTER 41   General Training 223

CHAPTER 42   Visiting Angels With Fur 227

CHAPTER 43   A Day At The Nursing Home. 235

CHAPTER 44   Romeo, Romeo, Where Are
             You? 239

CHAPTER 45   The Long Road Home. 247

CHAPTER 46   The Cornfields 251

CHAPTER 47   Welcome Home!. 257

CHAPTER 48   Who Is Training Who? 261

CHAPTER 49   Rio's Health 265

CHAPTER 50   Super Dogs! 270

CHAPTER 51   Smarty Pants!. 274

CHAPTER 52   The Gift. 281

CHAPTER 53   The Time Of My Life. 288

References 293

About the Author 295

Introduction

Sometimes, we love someone so much that when we lose them we are overwhelmed with grief and a sense of emptiness. We suffer shattering heartbreak, and I believe this is so because, in a way, that special someone does take a large part of our heart with them for their journey.

Much love for them, unanswered questions and regrets often remain, creating confusion that may never be resolved, but may remain stored within our deepest emotions. Some are so dear to us that when they leave, our life is altered dramatically, and we may never be the same ever again.

But if we are lucky enough, we are given another chance. We meet someone very special — a magical being, a joyful soul who helps make everything right again and gives us so much love, inspiration, and desire that we can go on. Thus, we come alive again.

This is my story…

CHAPTER 1

The Beginning

"Losing someone you love is never easy."

—Joni

Have you ever been so heartbroken, depressed, and in so much turmoil that you did not think you could go any lower?

Yes, I was.

And yes, I did think that.

One morning, I woke up and could not move. I lay in bed and discovered I could not move my arms or legs — it was as if they were detached from the rest of my body.

Perhaps my mind was awake, and the rest of me was still sleeping? I could think clearly, but physically felt nothing for about a minute. Then, thank goodness, feeling returned to my limbs and I was able to move again.

I got out of bed without enthusiasm.

The day seemed bleak. Unable to think of anything to look forward to doing that day, I began mechanically going through my morning ritual. I slowly dressed, then brushed my still thick but whitening blonde hair. What was happening to me? So many days I'd wake up and dread the thought of what the new day would bring.

My life was in chaos. I was overwhelmed, stressed, and my entire world seemed to be falling apart. My heart ached painfully from losing my only sister, Pat, a few months ago to a long, horrible battle with brain cancer, Aunt Jane to pneumonia last month, and now my beloved dog, Marly, from his silent battle with stomach cancer.

Life was so busy I did not have time to grieve and heal. My full-time job was very demanding, and since Pat's health had declined dramatically earlier last year, I had become Mom's primary caregiver.

Juggling my responsibilities was suddenly very difficult. I felt I could not keep up, as though I were treading water and losing the battle. I was physically and mentally drained.

Mom, my partner Joe, and Marly had kept me going through the tough times. They were my pillars, giving me the strength to take on every day's challenges. But now Marly was gone, and all too quickly.

While I was watching television and cuddling Marly in my arms, as we both so loved, Marly abruptly took a deep breath. It was his last. As quickly and quietly as cancer had taken him over, he left us. He did not appear to have any pain or discomfort and gave us no warning.

Although I did not think I could cry anymore after the passing of Pat and Aunt Jane, tears flowed like a stream from my eyes for my loyal buddy Marly, my first shepherd dog, my beloved Belgian Tervuren. Joe took the loss of Marly very hard, too.

Marly had always been our effervescent boy, with a big sparkle in his eye and the smile that stole our hearts. He was our water-loving boy who swam like a fish to catch the floating Frisbee we threw into the pool, the always on-duty, hardworking boy who trotted in circles around our guests with a grin on his face, nipping gently on their buttocks in good old-fashioned herding-dog style as he tried to round them up and bring them to us. He was the unpredictable boy who slept on his back, opened his eyes in surprise, and was so overjoyed to see me when I arrived home early from work one day that he peed on me like a classical garden fountain. Marly was also the swift little boy who once could run like the wind, chasing Frisbees, balls, and utility men who did not let us know they were coming.

We intermittently laughed at those fond memories as I cried hysterically, recalling so many sweet moments and fun times we had shared with Marly. Our hearts ached so.

Shaman, our German Shepherd rescue, took the loss of his best buddy Marly very hard and did a lot of sulking in the next days. We did our best to cheer him up, taking him for long walks and car rides. The extra attention and time together seemed to help him and us.

Mom also took Marly's loss hard. How she loved that charming boy! He was always the enchanting little elf who would smile at her, then climb gently and slowly like a sloth up onto the couch next to her, give her juicy kisses, then softly rest his head on her lap. He was always there to protect her from the bogeymen.

Mom was emotionally devastated from the loss of Pat, her oldest daughter (who had lived with her), then Aunt Jane (her sister-in-law) and now Marly was gone, too.

I tried to keep Mom's spirits up, keep her active and going places, and helped her with her housework and errands. Mom was tougher than we ever imagined. She held her head high and did her best to be strong and keep smiling.

She knew keeping busy was important, so she focused her time on the needs of family and friends, caring for

Pat's favorite pals, Bijou, an Australian Shepherd, and Gibran, a small All-American dog, and cheering on her favorite New York Yankees. Keeping busy helped the time pass and momentarily eased the pain.

CHAPTER 2

The First Belgian

"Dogs fill your heart and make your house a home."

—*Joni*

$\mathcal{M}$arly had joined our family 13 years before, a few months after Joe and I rescued Shaolin, a cheerful but lumbering black Labrador-Shepherd mix. Shaolin had stolen our hearts at the rescue when he put his paw through the bars of his kennel run every time we walked by, saying, "Pick me! Pick me!" So we did.

After rescuing Shaolin, we thought it would be good to have two dogs so they could keep each other company while we were at work. Joe had begun frequently traveling overseas for weeks at a time for his job, and the thought of having two large shepherd dogs at home for companionship and protection made me feel much more at ease.

We put a lot of effort into selecting Marly. We admired many dog breeds, but were not sure which one would be best for us, so we bought a few dog breed books and did a lot of homework about breed characteristics and personalities.

Joe, an engineer, required me to create a detailed checklist of the traits we wanted most in our next canine companion. After quite a bit of work, the list narrowed down to smart, easy to train, good watchdog and protector, loyal and friendly with family and friends, and not too many health issues.

We preferred a large dog, and one who did not drool very much. And, of course, we wanted a dog who fit our description of beautiful. You know the phrase, "You know it when you see it."

Lo and behold, topping the list was a herding breed we did not know much about, the Belgian Tervuren. We read that Tervuren are very intelligent, loyal, and all of the other things on our checklist, and the Tervuren in the photo books appeared so elegant and stunning.

We did more homework about the breed and agreed a Tervuren was the dog for us, so off we went in search of a puppy.

The American Belgian Tervuren Club, the breed's national club, referred us to Kate and Jeff from Connecticut who had just had a litter of Tervuren puppies. We called them and were delighted to discover that although many of their puppies were headed for the conformation show ring, they wanted to place some puppies with people like us who wanted a family member, not a show dog.

Kate and Jeff invited us to visit their home and meet their recent adorable puppy litter to see if any of their puppies were a good match with us. We were off to Connecticut! We couldn't wait to meet their puppies!

Kate and Jeff have been Tervuren breeders for many years. It was obvious to us that they love and take fantastic care of their dogs. Their pride was apparent as they introduced us to their new litter of puppies. The puppies were outside playing together, having fun, where we could observe their various personalities and make our selection. It was a hard choice. But one pup stood out.

Which puppy did we like best? The happiest, most active and rambunctious one, of course! The one who did not shy away from the other puppies, but was very confident and had a big personality. We named him Marly. We had to wait until Marly was old enough to leave his mother. Weeks went by, and when the time came, we drove back to Connecticut to pick him up. We were so excited to see him again!

Marly was such a delightful puppy, sleeping like an innocent little angel in my arms on the way home. I was in paradise.

My bliss lasted a couple of hours when, without warning, he burped and threw up his entire breakfast all over me. Ugh. Apparently Marly was car sick. He looked at me with sad eyes, as if to apologize.

We finally arrived home, looking forward to seeing Shaolin and having him meet our new family member. I also looked forward to a shower and change of clothes. Joe opened the door to the house and Shaolin ran out excitedly, tail wagging his body like any good black Labrador would do, so happy to see us. Then he saw the wiggling stranger in my arms.

Shaolin's expression instantly went from pure joy to pain and rejection. He stopped short, then abruptly did an about-face and stumbled away from me slowly, head drooping. He walked back into the house, clearly feeling rejected. Joe and I rushed after him, me holding Marly, to assure Shaolin that he was still our first love.

That was the beginning of Shaolin's life with Marly, but thankfully, their relationship quickly improved. They rapidly became the best of friends, Shaolin forgave us, and we became a happy and inseparable foursome.

Marly was full of energy and very curious about everything he encountered. Like all Tervuren, he always needed to be doing something. And when he became determined to do that "something," we learned quickly that he was very persistent in getting whatever he wanted.

It was good that we'd had several dogs in our lives previously, because Tervuren, or Tervs, as they are well known, are not for the first-time dog owner. As all Terv owners know or learn very quickly, if we do not give these smart Belgians a job, they will find one on their own, and we may not like the job they select.

We hugged and played a lot with Marly and Shaolin, but to their disappointment, we both had to go to work, and I to night school. Several times during the school year I also had to cram for exams.

While studying, I kept Marly in a large training box next to me, where he could play with his toys and I could keep an eye on him. For a short time, Marly would happily entertain himself, and that usually worked pretty well for my studying purposes, but not always.

Marly loved all his toys, but was especially taken with a large, fluffy wooly ball Kate had given him. One day, while I was studying next to Marly, the clever boy learned he could make the ball even fluffier by nipping and pulling at it with his teeth. Soon the one large ball transformed into dozens of fluffy little balls, which Marly managed to fling out of the training box and scatter around the room. What fun he was having!

Marly then noticed that he got Mum's attention while doing this.

"She really likes this too!" he thought, so he worked all the harder at making and flinging the little balls at me and around the room.

When Marly grew tired of chewing on his toys, his next mission was to escape from his training box so he could play directly with Mum. I was much more interesting and animated than his toys.

Marly's most active escapee moments seemed to coincide with the precious last few hours I had to cram for exams and desperately needed to focus. He would escape over and over again, and I would spend many minutes trying to catch him and return the wiggling boy back to his box each time.

In retrospect, I must admit Marly obviously (and very wisely) believed it was much more important, for both him and me, to get my attention and engage me in play-time with him, than for him to stay quietly in the box and watch me just sit there oddly staring at a book. Shaolin, lying comfortably in his cushy bed, very well-behaved I might add, always seemed to smile, clearly finding Marly's behavior very amusing. It was obvious Shaolin thought, "That is what you get in return for getting another pup!"

Our lives began to change in so many ways with these two happy and high-spirited boys, and it was all positive. Marly and Shaolin brought much joy and love to us, and we adored being around them every moment we could. We took them for long walks in our neighborhood and local parks, for long car rides to the seashore for walks in the sand, and to visit Mom and my sister Pat. Both were avid dog lovers and instantly fell in love with them, enjoyed their antics and happy personalities and always looked forward to seeing them.

CHAPTER 3

That Belgian Magic

"There is nothing like the magic and unconditional love that a dog brings into your life."

—Joni

*M*arly was remarkably clever and funny, and always seemed to be up to something. He gave us so many fond memories, that to this day I still laugh at his amusing antics.

Marly was still a young puppy when we invited good friends over for a barbeque dinner on our backyard deck. As a new puppy Dad and Mum, Joe and I kept a close watch over Marly and kept him right by our sides; even so, part way through dinner we noticed Marly was gone.

We could not find him anywhere. We went crazy searching everywhere for him for more than an hour, thinking he had escaped from the fenced-in yard some-how. Then, to our immense relief, one of our friends found Marly sleeping peacefully under our wooden deck, right below our feet, where he must have been all that time!

Time passed quickly; Marly turned two. When we began having problems with our landline phone, Joe called the telephone company, who said they would come to check out the problem but could not commit to a specific day. Several days later, Joe came home from work and saw the company's truck parked down the street, but didn't think anything of it because the truck was several houses away.

As Joe did every day when he arrived home, he let Shaolin and Marly out into our fenced-in backyard so they could do their business and run. And run they did! They took off at top speed towards their potty area in the back of the yard, with Joe jogging after them.

Seconds later, Joe heard a deep voice yell, "DOGS!!!!"

Joe hurried past the trees in the back of the yard to see four huge, football player-sized men leaping over our four-foot chain-link fence as if they were Olympic athletes in a hurdling event!

When Joe asked why they did not call to let us know they would be here today to work on the phone line, they told him they had left a message for us on our answering machine.

"But you turned off the power to the phone, so we didn't know we had a message," Joe replied. They all laughed heartily.

"All's well that ends well," they said.

A very smart boy and a quick learner, one of the jobs Marly assigned himself as he got older and very responsible was to be Joe's perfect alarm clock, one with guaranteed results. Marly somehow learned to wake Joe up a couple of minutes before Joe's alarm clock was set to go off. It was as if Marly had his own internal alarm clock.

Marly would come to Joe's side of the bed and plop his chin on the bed next to him. If that did not wake Joe immediately, Marly would lift his head and put his chin back on the bed with a bit more gusto, then shake his head back and forth impatiently, each time nuzzling closer and closer to Joe. If Joe still did not wake up, Marly would snake his nose further under the sheets until he found Joe's bare skin. Then Marly would nudge his cold wet nose against Joe's skin, causing Joe to wake immediately and jump up in surprise.

We have many joyful memories of Marly and Shaolin together. They were inseparable best buddies and very happy pups. Their favorite activities were playing catch with a tennis ball and Frisbee, and racing each other to catch them first.

Marly and Shaolin loved to play Frisbee in all kinds of weather. They enjoyed very cold weather and running and jumping in the snow to catch the Frisbee, then running back to us, side by side, sharing the Frisbee in their mouths.

They both had so much fun when retrieving that they did not know when enough was enough for them. We had to stop throwing the ball and Frisbee for their own good so they would not get overheated. But when we did that, they both would stare at us with their anxious big brown eyes, tails wagging their bodies, and begging for, "Just another one, please!"

Both dogs had long fur, so on hot summer days they enjoyed swimming in our in-ground pool to cool off. Shaolin, fearlessly and without any hesitation, always did a running start and dove into the pool on the deepest end, making a loud splash. Marly, "Mr. Elegance," preferred to gracefully walk down the pool steps into the shallow side, then proceeded to do a few small circular laps.

Marly especially made us laugh when, to our surprise on a few extremely hot days, he walked slowly and stealthily to the pool, looking over his shoulders first to the left, then to the right, to see if Joe was watching him. He wanted to sneak a quick dip to cool off and knew Joe might disapprove, depending on the time of day. Marly knew I would gladly let him take a dip in the pool to cool off, no matter what time of day, but we tried to keep that a secret from Joe so none of us would get into trouble.

On hot days like these, Marly wanted a quick swim and could not see both of us watching him with amusement through the kitchen window, so he proceeded to slowly walk down the steps and into the pool in true Marly fashion to do a few laps. Once he finished his laps and had cooled off enough, he climbed the steps out of the pool and started shaking the water off.

A few times, much to Marly's surprise, he found Joe and me there to greet him when he reached the top step of the pool. He always looked startled, but quickly gave us a huge grin to say, "Hi!" in his impish Marly way.

Then he'd get a quizzical look on his face as we laughed, as if he were saying, "Pool, what pool? I did not go for a swim. What made you think that?" We'd smile and giggle as the water dripped off our soaking wet dear buddy while we gave him a hug.

CHAPTER 4

Shaolin and Marly

*"Though you will never get over the loss of a dog or
other loved one, a new best furry friend will distract
you, keep you going and get you out and about."*

—Pat

Our happy memories led to sad ones as we remembered how we lost Shaolin. Time had flown by very quickly, and the time we spent with Marly and Shaolin made it all the more enjoyable. I finished school and got a new job, and Joe continued traveling. Then one very hot summer, Shaolin lost his appetite. I took him to our vet right away.

Shaolin was diagnosed with liver cancer. The vet said Shaolin was in no pain and gave him a couple of weeks to live.

One evening a few weeks later, Joe, Marly, and I went to sleep next to Shaolin on our basement floor. Shaolin wanted to sleep there as his condition worsened, because the basement was cool and dark, so we all joined him to be with him, take care of him, and so he would not be lonely. Sometime during the evening, Shaolin passed away peacefully by my side.

Losing Shaolin was a huge heartbreak. I could not do much but cry for days. Shaolin had been a best friend, and always a first-class gentleman we could take anywhere. He traveled with me to visit family and friends, to community events, to 9/11 ceremonies, and even to our local assemblyman's fundraisers.

Marly was saddened by the loss of his furry best friend, so we did our best to keep him busy and happy, taking him for his favorite long walks and rides to the park and the shore. Though we knew there would be an adjustment period, we wanted to get Marly a new canine companion quickly so he would have company while we were at work and would not feel alone.

We rescued Shaman, a long-haired black German Shepherd. Shaman was a shy older dog, much lower key than Shaolin. He was very gentle and beautiful, both inside and outside. We loved his endearing personality, as did everyone he met, and he was strikingly handsome with his long, black silky coat. When we walked down the street with him, people stopped to meet and greet him — even passersby in their cars — wanting to find out more about this good-looking, big black shepherd. It helped us socialize him and helped him build confidence.

Shaman was so happy to be with us. He was grateful we rescued him, and loved his new "leash on life" as our best friend and part-time couch potato. He most of all enjoyed going for walks and rides and hanging out with us.

Marly and Shaman soon became best buddies, and both continued to carry on the tradition of swimming in the pool for the next few years. But unlike Shaolin and Marly's love of Frisbees and balls, Shaman was not much interested in playing with either of them. He would run all out and catch the Frisbee or ball, but then would run away from us with them in his mouth, laughing and saying, "Come chase me! You did not want this and threw it away, so why should I give this back to you?"

Too soon, it was Marly's turn to move on to Rainbow Bridge. We had treasured our happy days and nights with this beloved boy by our side. He had been so full of life, so smart, so devoted to us, and such a joy to be with. When Marly passed quickly from stomach cancer, I cried so hard. We were sure going to miss him. Shaman and Mom, like us, took the passing of Marly very hard.

We gave Marly a funeral many would envy. While Joe dug his grave in our backyard, I read heartwarming dog love poems, sang, cried, and planted flowers on his grave, next to Shaolin. We will always miss Marly's big heart, his sweet personality, amazing Terv intelligence, loyalty and devotion, and his willingness to learn and do anything with us.

∞

Although it was only days after Marly's passing, we found it strangely quiet at home. It seemed unbearable, without Marly's strong, active, and loving presence. The house seemed so empty. Above the deafening silence, I heard my sister Pat's voice telling me what she had told me many times.

"When your dog passes away, the best thing to do is to get another one right away, whether a puppy or an older dog — because the new dog will distract you, keeping you very busy as you both try to learn about each other, and she/he will open up a new place in your heart to make a space for all the love they give you. This new, enthusiastic love they give you will ease the pain of your loss. Though you will never get over the loss of a dog or other loved one, a new best furry friend will distract you and keep you going and get you out and about."

I decided to follow Pat's advice.

We wanted another Tervuren. We loved Marly's fun personality, intelligence, and loyalty to us. We loved all the joy and excitement he brought into our lives and desperately wanted another dose of that Belgian magic.

I contacted Marly's breeders, Kate and Jeff, and told them Marly had passed. They were very sad because they loved Marly too, but told us we had taken really good care of Marly through all these years. He had lived the longest of all of the pups in his litter.

I asked Kate if they were planning a litter, or if she had a pup who would make me laugh and smile — I really needed that. I needed happy energy in the house, and I knew a new Terv would certainly bring that to us.

"No," Kate replied. They were not breeding right now, unless we wanted to wait several months for their next litter. "But we have a one-year-old dog, a handsome male named Zane Grey."

Zane was named after an American author.

"Interesting name," I thought. I Googled and learned that Zane Grey wrote adventure novels and stories about the American West and nature. Working in the environmental field, I hoped that if Zane Grey loved nature, he must have had an environmental side, so maybe this was a sign Zane and I were meant to be.

"You can have Zane if you like him. He will certainly make you laugh and smile. Do you want to meet him?"

"Sure!" I excitedly said.

"Great! There's a dog show in Edison, New Jersey, not far from you, in a couple of weeks. We will bring him with us," Kate replied.

"I cannot wait to meet you, Zane!" I was so excited.

Kate, Jeff, and Zane were coming down to the Raritan Center in Edison for the annual March American Kennel Club dog show weekend. We would meet them there. We hoped Zane would like us and would get along well with Shaman, despite the large age difference between them.

CHAPTER 5

Nice to Meet You, Zane and Rio!

*"Bringing a dog into your life can change your life in
so many positive ways."*

—*Joni*

The day to meet Zane came, and Joe and I were
very excited. We were happy to see Kate and Jeff;
after our greetings, Jeff went outside to get Zane.
Suddenly, there he was.

Zane Grey.

A proud-looking dog, with a stately stance and very
alert eyes, head up and tail wagging, clearly excited as
he watched the other show dogs go by. He was strikingly
handsome, elegant even, with a black face and overcoat
with light cream (almost white) tail and legs, and a unique
beige circle that ran from his lower back to his tail, amidst
his black top coat. His tail was mostly beige with a black
spot right in the middle.

Zane was very attentive to Kate, Jeff, and the other
dogs passing by, but was aloof towards us. Unlike Shaolin

who had kissed everyone he met, Zane did not seem to notice us and did not care that we were there.

"We just met and obviously do not know each other, so there is no reason for him to give us attention," I told myself.

Zane was very interested in all the other dogs at the show and what they were doing, but could not care any less about Joe and me. He had absolutely *zero* interest in us.

But Zane was extremely handsome and seemed to have a nice temperament and personality, so we asked Kate and Jeff if we could walk him around the convention center and interact with him. Maybe he would warm up and pay a little attention to us. Kate and Jeff sent us on our way so we could become friends.

We walked around the inside of the convention building a few times. Zane appeared comfortable in the busy show atmosphere and even seemed to know his way, leading us around the show. He seemed to be smiling and excited to be there amongst hundreds of magnificent show dogs. I found him to be very confident and quite an intriguing young man.

After an hour with Zane, we returned to Kate and Jeff.

"Do you like him?" they asked.

"Yes, he's absolutely lovely," we said, "but we do not know if he likes us."

Kate told us not to worry. We could take him on a trial basis and see what happens.

"Zane is a really good boy and lots of fun and he will certainly warm up to you," she said, but warned us he did not like car rides.

"If Zane does not work out, not to worry. We would gladly take him back," Kate reminded us.

"We would love to give Zane a try."

"Great! We'll give you his toys and food from the car," Kate said, "but there is just one condition … if you take Zane, you *must* show him in the conformation ring."

"Show him? I have never shown anything before," I told her, laughing.

"That doesn't matter. Just take some conformation lessons, and go out and have lots of fun," Kate said, smiling.

"So, do you want him?"

We nodded our heads in approval.

"We would love to take him home," we said, though I did not have a clue what conformation lessons and shows were.

Jeff brought us Zane's toys and food and got ready to leave.

"Have fun with showing," Kate said with a big smile.

"Okay," I replied, not knowing at all what I was getting into. Saying thank you and goodbye, I led Zane outside to my car, hoping in my heart he would grow to like us. We had our first success when Zane jumped without hesitation into the back of my Prius. So much for him not liking car rides.

"Maybe he really is an environmentalist. He seems to love my Prius hybrid," I thought.

Little did we know Zane and I were embarking on a life-changing adventure for both of us, a magical journey I will always treasure. Zane would change my life in ways I could never have foreseen. And I would do the same for him.

∞

Zane was a unique name, but I had a difficult time getting used to it. Although many people liked the name, I was not sure about it and certainly did not want to call him Zane or Zany in the show ring.

A dictionary defined "zany" as, "... surprisingly different and a little strange, and therefore amusing and interesting." I did not want his name to suggest that he was strange or funny in an odd way, so we changed his name from Zane to Rio, a name we had always liked.

Enter Rio! What an exciting, lively name! It prompted images of travel to new exotic places, lively music and dancing, and thrilling things to do. Rio de Janeiro. Rio Grande. Rio, meaning a "river," perhaps an exciting journey. That is his name!

We brought Rio to his new home. Now older and set in his ways, Shaman did not welcome Rio at first, and immediately staked his claim to his favorite bed. His first thoughts were clear, "Here comes a hotshot show dog who is going to invade my home, steal my family, and will want to be the alpha dog."

But that was not the case. Yes, Rio was very different than Shaman. Rio was young, energetic, and from a show-world family, and very sociable, independent and smart, with a strong personality.

Rio saw the world as his playground — he wanted to get out and explore it, not sit on a couch. Shaman was very much the opposite. What he had gone through before we rescued him we did not know, but we were spoiling him, and he was greatly enjoying his senior years. He did not want to lose our attention.

Rio was very nice to Shaman. All he wanted was equal rights and opportunity in our household, to learn and keep busy all the time, and most of all to love and be loved and cherished.

Once that was clear, Shaman and Rio accepted each other, learned to love and respect each other, and even relied on each other. Unfortunately, Shaman was already up in years, and in retrospect, possibly ill, because he was slowing down significantly. In just over a year, he passed over the Rainbow Bridge.

CHAPTER 6

Entering the Show World

"Make new goals, commit to those challenges and shoot for the stars!"

—Joni

"Wh

at exactly is a conformation show?" I wondered. Searching the Internet, I found the American Kennel Club site and learned that "conformation" is the official name for a dog show. At these shows, dogs are evaluated by a judge as to how closely they "conform" to their breed's standard. Those dogs who are closer to their breed standard will most likely produce puppies who continue to meet the breed standard.

I read the Belgian Tervuren breed standard again, to understand Rio and the breed better from the show ring perspective. Some words stood out to me based on what I already knew of Rio: proud, lively, unquestionably masculine, and alert.

Yes, Rio is all of that.

Like Marly, Rio is certainly *proud* to be a Tervuren, holding his head high and standing so stately and sure of himself. He looks proud when he meets a new canine friend, at which time he confidently aligns his legs in a perfect stack position and holds his head up high with his entire face smiling, eyes glistening, and tail wagging. (Stacking, as I would soon learn in the show ring, is a term used in dog shows that refers to getting your dog to stand in a way that best shows his/her attributes to the judge. Stacking can be done with physical guidance by the dog's handler, or by verbal commands.)

Rio is also very *lively* and effervescent with an abundance of energy, and is very unpredictable because he is always on the move. I began keeping Rio busy with walks and long rides, and as time went on, with the conformation classes I had promised Kate we would take, as well as other types of training classes. If it is not a show or training day, Rio still wants to do training or go for a walk, so I do my best to be creative with his activities to keep his mind and body active.

When I have apparently slacked off on my activities for the day, Rio has reminded me on a number of occasions of the fact that once you get a Tervuren, you must give them a job, and if you do not, they will create their own activities and you may not like what they decide to do.

Many times Rio made up his mind to do something, and despite our earnest efforts to the contrary, he just did what he wanted. Rio obviously believes, "It is better to ask for forgiveness later with my handsome grin or 'oops' expression, than to ask anyone for permission to do something first."

Rio is joyful and happy to be alive, living by the words Carpe Diem — making the most of the present and not worrying about the future. He lives vivaciously in the "now" moment.

He is also *unquestionably masculine* — a ladies' man, smiling and saying, "hello," when he sees a female Belgian (or any female dog for that matter). Rio's tail wags so excitedly it literally wags his body, and he grins so charmingly, eyes sparkling at each lady jewel, young or old. He often stretches out one front paw gently to the lovely jewel, asking sweetly, "Would you like to be my friend and play with me, beautiful lady?"

Rio is such a gentleman, and very polite, too. As such, he looks confused and quizzical when a gal ignores him, gives him sass, or flips her body around 360 degrees in a Tervuren circle. Rio has never been bred, but hope always springs eternal for him.

He is also very *alert*. *Nothing* gets past him. He hears every sound — from the far end of the hallway at home, he hears the chair creak when I stand up to get something in the farthest room. From several feet away, he hears the silent footsteps of a chipmunk trying to pass him as he rests on the patio. He even hears my car coming down the street long before the garage door starts to open.

Because Rio has so many of the characteristics listed in the American Kennel Club's Belgian Tervuren standard, I felt confident he would quickly earn his Championship title. I was in for quite a surprise.

Rio grew up quickly and speedily adapted to his new life in our home. He became even more confident and devoted to us once he began to understand the rules of the house and our daily and weekly schedules. He bonded with us quickly, learning that we were the provider of all good things … yummy food, belly rubs, long walks, and rides in the car to take him to fun places like training, shows, and to see his girlfriends, who Rio seemed to find everywhere we went. We quickly fell in love with this darling boy.

Family and friends loved our new bubbly boy, especially Mom. They thought it was pretty cool that Rio was a show dog and I was going to show him (except for Mom, who was a bit skeptical about the entire show scene).

Friends suggested I watch the movie *Best In Show* to see what I was getting myself into. We did, and it was hilarious. I thought — at least hoped — that the show ring would not really be exactly like that.

I started doing research about the conformation show ring and to find a training school that offered conformation classes to fulfill Kate's request that I learn how to show Rio. That autumn, off I went with Rio to start conformation training in between working, helping Mom, and everything else. Training and hanging out with Rio proved to be a much-needed, happy distraction for me.

Rio and I started conformation lessons at St. Hubert's Dog Training School, where I had previously taken all our dogs for basic obedience training. It is a very well-known and reputable local dog-training facility. At the time, I did not know much about dog training other than the basic commands they teach in an introductory obedience course such as sit, down, and stay.

Conformation training was a new experience and life-changing for both me and Rio. This is where Rio became my first show dog and I became his owner-handler, and both he and I grew up in so many ways. And so, our journey of a lifetime together began.

CHAPTER 7

Let the Shows Begin!!

*"Put your heart into your goals and desires, work
hard, and you will succeed."*

—Joni

Rio and I were very excited to start evening conformation lessons. Rio was thrilled to go for a
nice car ride every week to meet so many new
dogs and make more friends, and it was an honor for me
just to think of possibly entering an American Kennel
Club conformation show someday with Rio by my side.

We were very lucky to get into the St. Hubert's classes
because they always filled quickly, and most of all, because
leading them was the best teacher in the world for us,
Stacey. She was always cheerful, encouraging, and supportive, with the patience of a saint.

Most of our fellow classmates had been taking lessons
with Stacey for years with many different show dogs, most
were breeders, and all were very accomplished handlers.

Stacey's students won top placements in conformation shows frequently, often winning best of breed, so it was quite an honor to be training with them. It was exciting to watch them sail gracefully around the ring and stack their dogs perfectly. They made the training ring at St. Hubert's look like the Westminster Dog Show.

Stacey guided us with great skill and care.

"Take them all around once."

"Now line up your dogs."

"Stack your dogs."

"First dog up for examination here."

"Out and back!"

"Take your dog around once."

One by one we went through the show routine, then escorted our dogs around the ring again. I learned about the rules of the show ring, including the proper etiquette to be followed, and about gaiting — moving around the show ring with your dog at the most appropriate speed so as to show your dog in the best position. This is when judges appraise your dog's movement. Add to that stacking, standing for examination, and many different ways to exhibit Rio. I learned a lot about grooming, though I have never seemed to master it. And once we started showing, I would learn a lot about patience and humility!

I studied the American Kennel Club breed standard for the Belgian Tervuren again, now with a clearer understanding of what would be expected in the show ring. A dog "... elegant in appearance ... proud carriage ... gait: lively and graceful ...."

Ah, yes, that is Rio!

I was getting very excited to show Rio, as he had matured more and was handsomely beautiful.

I did have my challenges, including running gracefully around the ring. How can I best make Rio look good? How should I hold the show lead? Does Rio look better with a short or long lead? Should I hold my arm close to him, or held up high like I am showing off the Crown Jewels?

Should I give Rio a plain black lead that matches the black part of his coat, or one with rhinestones to accentuate his multi-color coat? How do I get him to trot and not pace, which as he gets older, he wants to do more and more?

"Practice makes perfect," I have been told. So we practiced, practiced, and practiced some more.

The weeks went by quickly. We finished several rounds of Stacey's classes and learned a lot. After running around the training ring hundreds of times, I started to feel comfortable in what we were doing and was anxious to give the show ring a try. I decided to start showing Rio in the conformation ring soon at local shows, "local" meaning within three hours of our home.

I called Kate for advice. Kate explained how to do online electronic entries. That done, we entered our first show weekend. The categories of class dogs included Puppy, Twelve-to-Eighteen-Month, Bred by Exhibitor, American Bred and Open Dog classes. Kate recommended we enter Rio as Open Dog, as Rio was too old for the Puppy or Twelve-to-Eighteen Month classes, and we did not qualify for the Bred by Exhibitor category.

I found our first show. About a year after getting Rio, I was going to show Rio at the Edison American Kennel Club show, the very place where we first met Rio. We entered the Open Dog class all four days of the show. Rio took well to the show ring, as a very well-behaved boy with a marvelous disposition, and a nice gait and stack. We tried very hard to mimic everything we had learned in class.

Rio did not earn any points, but earned placement ribbons, and with what I thought was some luck, placed ahead of some handlers who had shown for many years. I was ecstatic!

That was the beginning of our show life and our show journey together. After that weekend, I signed Rio up for every conformation show within three hours of home, hoping one of the judges would like Rio best, and there would be enough dogs entered for Rio to win Winners Dog and earn some points, and better yet, a three-point major.

To earn an American Kennel Club Championship, a dog has to earn a total of fifteen points, with at least two three-point majors. To earn a point in the Tervuren ring, a dog has to win over the other class dog entered (assuming there is one other dog entered); for two points, a dog has to win over two other class dogs entered. The top dog in the class dog competition is known as the Winners Dog; the top bitch in the bitch class is known as the Winners Bitch.

To earn a three-point major, a dog has to be Winners Dog by winning over three other class dogs, or do a "cross-over,"' by being Winners Dog, and then have the judge select him as Best of Winners over the class bitch who won a three-point major at that show. One can also win four and five-point majors, all depending on how many other dogs and bitches are entered.

This applied for the Belgian Tervuren showing in New Jersey and some other states at the time, not all around the country. Some areas of the United States had more or less Tervs showing, so their point schedules varied accordingly.

Interestingly, the point schedules determined by the American Kennel Club for other breeds often varied considerably from those applicable to Tervuren, with some breeds requiring a win over a dozen or more dogs to earn a major because of the frequent high-entry numbers.

Tervuren handlers came to New Jersey to compete from New York, Pennsylvania, Connecticut, Massachusetts, and other states much farther away. As Tervuren are usually very devoted to their owners and prefer to be handled by them rather than professional handlers, most handlers were also "owner-handlers." Many of these owner-handlers were also long-time breeders who were very seasoned handlers.

They knew what they were doing from decades of experience, and some were accomplished judges themselves. It was thrilling to watch them glide around the ring so gracefully with their Tervuren and keep their dogs' complete attention while stacking. Often competing in our ring was the Number Two Tervuren male dog in the country, with a very full, gorgeous coat, handled by a top professional handler. As such, our competition was usually top-notch and tough.

About that time, I was introduced through a friend at work to a co-worker, Cathy, a veteran of the conformation show ring, having shown and bred magnificent Boston Terriers for many years. She always has several beautiful female Boston Terriers.

This was my first introduction to the lovely Boston Terrier breed, known as the American Gentleman, which originated in the United States. Bostons are small when compared to Belgians, usually 25 pounds or less, with a short coat. Rio weighs about 65 pounds, and with his long double-coat, looks quite large when standing next to a Boston. Bostons are adorable and fun to watch at the shows.

Most of the time Cathy hires professional handlers to handle her girls in the ring. She has been very successful with them, earning their Grand Championships at the highest of levels. Cathy taught me a lot about showing, and I am very grateful to her. Not only did she help me understand the rules of the sport, but she helped me with etiquette and a lot of administrative requirements.

Cathy explained that sometimes showing gets very competitive, as many activities in life do, and some competitors try to win at all costs. She told me stories, many of them just too funny, of what people have done to try to sway a judge to get a win.

She also explained there are many people who have the financial ability to hire the best professional handlers, send their dogs off to shows anywhere in the United States, Canada, Europe, and elsewhere, and take out full-page advertisements in dog magazines on a regular basis.

Clearly, dog showing can be very expensive, as well as competitive, and a lot may be at stake. But, as I learned, there are magical times when owner-handlers with beautiful dogs do win over the popular Champions handled by professional handlers.

Cathy and I have shared many fun times at local shows and at Westminster. It is very important to have friends like Cathy in the sport who can mentor you, with whom you can share memorable show times, and also give them assistance in return.

The American Kennel Club also had a formal mentoring program for people new to the conformation ring. I contacted the program and was assigned to an active judge who was very pleasant and answered many questions I had.

Kate and Jeff were always happy to answer any questions about the show ring and grooming, as were many other Belgian Tervuren owners and handlers. Some owners and handlers of the other Belgian breeds, the Belgian Sheepdog and Malinois, and handlers of other breeds, were eager to give me advice about grooming and ring work. They were very encouraging and helpful to me as a new handler.

I made a lot of friends, and we often chatted and cheered each other on. Rio made a lot of friends himself, both canine and human, eager to charm many hearts with his endearing disposition. How he loved to flirt with the Belgian ladies!

I taught Rio that when I say, "Showtime," it means we are going for a long drive to a really cool place where we will run around the ring and have fun, then afterward, he can play and flirt with the other dogs. As such, Rio always rushes to the door in the morning when I say, "Today we are going to Showtime!" How he looks forward to these days and cannot wait to jump in my car for the ride!

Rio has a grand time at the shows. Running around the ring a few times and stacking is a small price to pay for meeting up with his girlfriends and buddies. Rio is always in heaven at the shows, wagging his tail, more than most dogs, I may add, with a charming sparkle in his eyes and a grin on his face. I am proud to have this fine gentleman as my best friend and partner in the show ring.

CHAPTER 8

Trials and Tribulations

"Don't ever give up on your dreams."

—Joni

Although we were having fun, at first we went home without winning anything. Despite everyone's helpful hints, sometimes it seemed we would never get any points. Not only was the competition very stiff, many times we were the only entry, so even though we were blessed to be honored with Best of Breed, there was little opportunity to earn points in our breed competition. We did not even think of getting a major win — that seemed impossible.

Some days I felt frustrated because Rio had shown very well against his competition, yet the judge did not select him over the other dogs. It did not seem to matter what some of the other dogs did. A couple of dogs, in different shows, growled viciously and snapped at Rio in the show ring. I was told that when a dog did that, the reactive or aggressive dog should be disqualified.

But they were not. Instead, the judge selected them over Rio, and they earned points, even Best of Breed.

It did not matter that other dogs kept their ears back, or if the other dogs were not well behaved like Rio. Some dogs even jumped up on the judge. And they all won over my Rio.

Though I sometimes felt disappointed, and had my share of teary moments, I refused to stop showing, even though my family, especially Mom, strongly encouraged me to stop. I enjoyed being in the ring with Rio and having fun with him at the shows. I needed this, as it was an enjoyable diversion from the deepening sadness I still felt from my family losses. Being in the show ring with Rio gave me an exciting activity to look forward to and made me feel happy, even if for a short time.

I, like Rio, greatly enjoyed making new friends at the shows. I encourage all new handlers to get out there and show their dogs and build the wonderful relationships with them that the show ring can help provide. Additionally, you can make a lot of wonderful life-long friends.

Most handlers and judges we met were very professional and nice. But as I was warned, not everything in life is always perfect. Some competitors do try unfair tactics to win at times. You should be prepared for that. But those times for me were few and far between.

One time, a fellow handler pointed out to me that, on a couple of occasions, a more seasoned handler had tried to take advantage of my naiveté in the show ring. Apparently, knowing how Rio loves to flirt with the bitches and would just about lose his mind and focus if he sniffed one, the handler kept bringing her bitch as near to Rio as possible while the class dogs were in line waiting to enter the ring. Later, in the ring for Best of Winners, she ran her bitch right up against Rio's side after they did their run around the ring, resulting in a very distracted boy.

To my surprise, Rio did a very nice job despite this, and the judge gave him Best of Winners and a three-point major over the bitch anyway.

Another time, Rio was the only Tervuren showing, and he was awarded Best of Breed. This was the first time Rio ever earned Best of Breed, so I was very excited to have the opportunity to enter the group ring with him. We waited anxiously in line with the other Herding Group Best of Breed winners, ready to enter the ring. One of the professional handlers, not knowing who I was in my new suit, may have assumed I was a professional handler.

The judge called us into the ring. The handlers in line in front of us started running into the ring with their dogs, but this professional handler, standing in line in front of me by the entry gate to the ring with his dog, just stood there partially blocking the entrance for several seconds and did not enter the ring. Instead, he turned around and walked slowly behind me toward the middle of the line, causing a large gap in the running.

The judge called out to all the handlers outside of the ring, wanting to know what was going on and where the rest of the dogs were. We all hurried into the ring, and the group judging continued. Maybe what that handler did was not unusual, but it appeared to a friend that he tried to make me look unprofessional.

At a different show, there were only two Tervuren entered in our Open Dog class. The other exhibitor and I stacked our dogs for the judge's inspection after we'd taken them once around the ring. To my surprise, the judge came over to Rio unusually quickly and abruptly leaned over him, causing him to be a bit startled. No judge had ever done that to him before.

Rio looked at her curiously, asking, "Why are you trying to frighten me, Ma'am?" and put his ears back. The judge proceeded to smile and award the ribbon to the other class dog, but first explained to me that Rio was going to bite her, did I not see that? No, I did not, and I would have been very surprised, because that is not Rio's temperament. Rather, he is one of the friendliest — perhaps the friendliest — Tervuren I have ever seen. But I could not say that to the judge, and even if I did, I knew doing so would get us nothing good.

Though these random incidents happened to us, they were rare. Overall, during our time showing in the conformation ring, the handlers and judges were very professional and wonderful to show with, making for an incredible experience and sweet memories.

Time went on, and although Rio did a nice job in the ring, we still were not earning any points. I knew I was not very lucky at this, but I would not give up, despite our lack of wins. Although I was warned this would be the norm for most handlers and dogs, and that it could take a long time to finish a dog's Championship, at first I became frustrated because we tried so hard. I began to think my handsome show dog deserved a better handler than I. I believed it was my fault Rio was not winning. I am not a graceful runner, and at times a bit klutzy, having fallen once in the ring after my shoe got stuck on the rubber floor matting.

Although I hired an excellent professional handler for a few shows, we had no better luck. Rio did not want to work for him, and not for anyone but me, so I continued to show Rio. With time, I learned a lot about humility and just moved on and entered more shows.

I continued to try my best. Rio was, in my mind, just as beautiful as many of the other dogs. He had a very nice gait and a more stable and cheerful disposition than many dogs we competed against. Although he has more of a long, European muzzle than many of the American Belgians, Europe is where the breed originated, and I was told by a number of Tervuren handlers that is how the dogs historically should look. Many Tervuren bred by

American breeders have a slightly different look, often with a broader muzzle and much lighter coat without a lot of black.

My family continued to encourage me to stop showing Rio in the conformation ring, but I would not give up showing my dear boy. Rio had so much fun at the shows and tried so hard to please me.

I believed Rio was a Champion, and in my heart, I knew that Rio will always be my Best in Show. He deserved to earn his American Kennel Club Championship title. I was determined. Or should I say, I became "dogged?"

CHAPTER 9

Pat

"Love and cherish those that love you — enjoy every moment with them, because these moments are fleeting."

—Joni

My older sister Pat was a very happy and energetic child. She was extremely clever, like our older brother William, and often would drive him near crazy with her jokes and pranks. We had a large family with many aunts, uncles, cousins, grandparents, and lots of friends and neighbors. Pat loved them all, and they adored her.

Pat always helped everyone she could, especially with chores and gardening and at Aunt Jane's small farm, our grandparents' homestead. She took enormous pride in washing Dad's old Cadillac and helping him around the house with repairs and painting.

Pat especially loved her dogs and found a lot of joy in walking, training, and caring for them. As long as I can remember, she always had at least one dog, up until the day she died. She had a lot of fun picking out creative and meaningful names for them.

Pat's many canine friends included her first rescues, King I and King II. Xavier, an Afghan Hound, was next, followed by Zephyr, a white Russian Wolfhound, then two German Shepherds, Lee I and Lee II, who Pat fondly named for Liberace, whose theatrical performances and music she so loved. Her last two dogs were rescues, Gibran, named for her favorite poet Kahlil Gibran, and Bijou, an Australian Shepherd from a puppy mill, named for a word she always loved the sound of. She adored them all.

Very special to her was Xavier, the Afghan Hound. She was so proud when she and Dad brought him home. Pat told me she and Dad had met with Sunny Shay at Sunny's Grandeur Kennels, and they picked out Xavier for her. This was in the mid-sixties. Sunny had won Best in Show at the Westminster Dog Show in 1957 at Madison Square Garden with her beautiful dog Champion Shirkhan of Grandeur — the first time an Afghan Hound won Best in Show at Westminster. I found all that impressive, but did not understand at the time what it meant.

Xavier was a son of Champion Shirkhan of Grandeur, but was a family pet, not a show dog, and Pat was very proud of him. He was a golden-colored dog with a golden heart, and we loved him very much. We had a lot of fun with Xavier, and his favorite pastime was his long walks, even in the deep snow.

Pat grew into a gorgeous blonde, very graceful teenage girl. She became a Barbizon model trainee. She loved to watch the movies of the fifties and sixties and emulated the Hollywood movie stars. Attractive and elegant, she turned the heads of many people walking on the streets of New York City when we visited, and she got many whistles!

Pat was always in good shape from being constantly active, and very strong from weightlifting, exercising and playing sports at school and with the kids in our beloved Rahway, New Jersey neighborhood. As a tom-boy, she often played baseball, football, and other sports better than William and many of the neighborhood boys. She later joined a local semi-pro girls' softball team and became a successful pitcher and batter.

In her late teens, Pat started dating George, a dear long-time family friend from Rahway. He was a very tall, dark, and handsome gentleman and very kind. Pat and George were a pair for a while, but then George went to serve our country in the Vietnam War. Tragically, George returned from the war with issues from his horrific experiences, and was not the same person we had known, physically or mentally.

I did not understand what had happened to him, as I was only a young child during the war. I never knew how atrocious that war was until I recently started reading a book titled *Kill Anything That Moves*, the military order given to many of our young and innocent soldiers who were sent to Southeast Asia in our name.

About the time George left for Vietnam, my brother William was called to serve, but was excused and told he never had to report due to a serious and permanent hip injury sustained while playing high school football. Although he has the injury to this day, I thank God for it, as it may have saved his life.

Soon afterward, Pat's illnesses began, the first of them being manic depression. At times, Pat was so upset she would not come out of her bedroom for days except to get food. The doctors failed to diagnose it, and no one in our family circle knew anything about depression at the time, or thought about her mood swings after she popped out of them. We were just happy she was back to her joyful, fun self.

Following in the footsteps of our Dad with her artistic talent, Pat began to devote her time to her art. She created beautiful sketches and paintings of nature scenes, dogs and other animals, and whimsical Christmas Santas, snowflakes, and snow scenes. Dad assisted Pat with artistic advice and life for Pat and all of us was good. We were all happy together.

∞

Time passed quickly. William married Cynthia and moved to Pittsburgh to start a family. I met Joe and we moved in together in the summer of 1986. We were happy and excited to be starting new careers.

We looked forward to celebrating Christmas at our new townhouse at the end of the year, the first family party ever at our new home, to be followed with a big birthday celebration for Pat two days later. Being very close, our family loved to see each other every day during the holidays.

However, the joy of celebrating this holiday season as one big happy family was cut short.

Early in the morning after our Christmas party, Dad awoke, coughing with congestion. He took cold medicine and stayed up part of the night because he felt uncomfortable. William sat up with him.

Unaware of how Dad was feeling, Joe and I went to Mom and Dad's the next morning to continue the holiday festivities with Mom and Dad, William and Cynthia, and Pat and her friend Roberta.

Dad did not look well. He was pale, tired, and out of breath. Minutes later, Joe came into the kitchen and told me Dad had confided to him that he was starting to have pains in his arm and chest.

We immediately took Dad to the emergency room at our local hospital. After evaluating him, the doctors advised Dad had had a heart attack that morning, but assured us he would be okay after a short stay in the hospital. We spent the rest of the day with him until visiting hours were over.

As we said our prayers that night, we looked forward to seeing Dad the next morning. It was Pat's birthday, and we hoped to celebrate her birthday, as we did every year, with Mom and Dad.

Waking early the following morning, I called the hospital for an update on Dad's condition and was told he was doing well and eating breakfast. We were thankful. Not long after, the phone rang as we were on our way out the door. It was the hospital — Dad had just had a massive heart attack. They told us to hurry.

We rushed to the hospital, but arrived too late. Dad passed shortly after they called us. We were all devastated. This was not supposed to happen — Dad was only 73 years old.

Life without Dad was incomplete for our family and friends, to say the least. He was such a loving man, our best friend, and always caring and fun. Family and friends always relied on him for everything. He was a very good handyman, able to fix most everything around the house, including our cars. He was always willing to help our friends and family and loyally helped his sister, Aunt Jane, with weekly errands and fixing up the old family homestead. The life of every party, Dad was charming, and a very kind gentleman. He was always supportive, full of compliments for everyone, and always had a clever clean joke to tell.

Dad's passing was a huge loss for us, but it was the greatest loss for Mom. He was the love of her life for almost 50 years, her devoted husband, and father of her children. He was her forever love, her protector, her everything. With his passing, her life was changed dramatically.

It goes without saying that William, Cynthia, Joe, me, and Pat also missed Dad greatly. At the time, William and

Cindy were beginning their lives in Pittsburgh together and trying to start a family. I had just started night school, and Joe and I were getting established at our jobs. We regret to this day that we never were able to share our later successes with Dad or repay him for all he did for us. I know he would be very proud of all of us.

Pat took it particularly hard. She considered Dad her best pal, and quite simply, adored him. She had always been by his side. Dad passed away on Pat's birthday, and this affected her deeply then, and in the years to come. Never again could Pat celebrate her birthday with her old gusto and parties.

CHAPTER 10

Life After Dad

"Cherish your family, they are the only one you have."

—Joni

Several months after Dad passed, Pat developed muscle pains and was not feeling quite right. After many doctor visits, the doctors diagnosed her with multiple sclerosis.

Roberta (Pat's good friend) and the family took Pat to the best doctors they could find. She was treated with medications, vitamins and dietary changes and seemed to do pretty well, except that the frequent tingling in her arms and legs would not go away.

Over time, Pat lost feeling in her arms and legs, so she could not feel if an object was hot or cold, sometimes causing her to get burned. She developed a limp and sometimes lost her balance, but she got around and continued with her painting and writing.

Pat continued taking care of her new dog, Lee, but she had difficulty walking him because of her imbalance.

Over time, she began to feel tired nearly all day, perhaps from the medications. It was about this time that Pat began training Lee to help her with daily activities such as getting her the mail and newspaper after they were delivered.

A German Shepherd and a quick study, Lee learned to help Pat with many daily chores.

Pat dealt very well with her multiple sclerosis, and it seemed to stabilize. She went on with her life as a self-employed artist, earning income by selling her paintings. She was also a very good writer and had begun writing poetry and a children's book before she got ill. To supplement her income, she did miscellaneous jobs for our family, and for a time, worked part-time at a local restaurant chain.

Pat did not work enough hours at her formal employment to have health benefits nor earn Social Security and Medicare. As such, the only healthcare she had was Medicaid, so she was permitted to see only Medicaid doctors, which we sadly discovered meant there were limited doctors available to treat her.

When Pat had extensive pain and needed immediate help, she went to the emergency room at Rahway or another hospital. They would always see her and try to help her, but that had its disadvantages. The doctors did not know Pat's long and complex health history and changes in her health, so the best they could do was provide her with temporary help — painkillers.

∞

After Dad's death, we all helped Mom with her errands, doctor visits and maintaining her house. Her antidote to grieving as she adjusted to life without Dad was to keep busy, so we kept her active with day-to-day activities and family gatherings. Mom also reached out to the community, by joining the St. Mary's Church choir and taking night school classes at the local high school. The years flew by and the family changed quickly, keeping her busy.

William traveled from Pittsburgh with his wife Cindy to visit a few times each year, and they had a son and named him Zachary. But after a few years, William lost his job, and Cindy and he divorced. William was destroyed, having lost his life with his beloved wife, child, home, and job all in a very short time. He stayed in Pittsburgh to be close to Zach, but continued to come out to help Mom when he could. Mom adapted as best she could without Dad as the family evolved.

Time moved on. I graduated from college, went on to earn my juris doctor degree, and then started my first job in my new career. Life was extremely busy but exciting, and no day was the same.

Pat's multiple sclerosis was being treated, and her health was stable for many years. Roberta helped Pat greatly with her healthcare through the years, but they eventually went their own ways, and Pat moved back in with Mom. Mom was happy to have Pat home and deeply appreciated her companionship and assistance with her home, garden, and errands. Soon after Pat got settled in, along came dogs Gibran and Bijou.

Our cousin Ann, between jobs, helped Pat with her doctor's visits and errands. Pat, Mom, and I were so grateful for all her help. When Ann went back to work, George, Joe, and I helped more when we could, and at other times, Pat took her mobility scooter or public-assistance transit to get her doctor visits and errands done.

Life was good. Though it was increasingly difficult, it was so good for all of us to be together. Those were days I fondly remember.

Over time, as her doctors had predicted, Pat's condition slowly worsened, but she continued to help Mom and did her utmost to maintain a normal life. Pat was very tough and determined, and she went out most days to work in the garden or go shopping, with George, or on her scooter. She tried to adjust to her illnesses and would not give in to them.

Pat continued to see her doctors, concerned about her health decline, but they said the changes in her condition were because multiple sclerosis is a degenerative disease, thus it would just be a matter of time before it worsened and shortened her life. Her condition had always seemed to be under control thanks to medications and vitamins, but lately she was physically losing more muscle control, and mentally, she began losing interest in many things. That was unlike Pat, who had great passion for living each moment of the day.

Pat could no longer paint because her hand shook quite a bit, and her writing was no longer the pretty flowing script it once was. It was now shaky and slanted. She could no longer walk her dogs because of her worsening balance issues, so Mom hired someone to install a fence around the yard so the dogs could be let outside to run throughout the day.

I was very saddened when I called Pat one day, telling her the snow had just started to fall outside our home, to find she was not interested. Not long ago, Pat had loved snow so much that she would do a happy dance at the sight of the first snowflake. She was not the same Pat.

As time went on, Pat complained of other symptoms, such as a ringing in her ears, which the doctors attributed to tinnitus. Her head felt itchy at times, and she wondered if she had lice (she didn't) or a disease causing the itchiness. Then Pat's neck began to hurt her, to the extent it became difficult to hold up her head and she started wearing a neck brace. The doctors attributed all her new pains to arthritis.

Pat frequently took painkillers to ease the pain and sleeping pills to help her sleep. As a result of the sleeping pills, and perhaps a side effect from all the medications she was taking, Pat slept a lot, sometimes most of the day. Then, after sleeping all day, Pat stayed up much of the night. She used that quiet time to write letters to family and friends, especially cousins Ann, Chrissie, Pat, Barbara, Irene, and Sal, whom she loved very much.

Over time, Pat developed what appeared to be a rash of small red bumps all over her arms. The doctors tried but could not diagnose this. We wondered if this was another side effect from the many medications she was obediently taking.

As the year went on, Pat struggled more with walking. Her limp progressively worsened, as did her vision and balance, and she began to stumble and fall more frequently, even though she now walked with the assistance of a cane. At the end of the year, she sent a holiday card to Ann, saying this was probably the last Christmas card she would send. She seemed to know her end was approaching.

CHAPTER 11

System Failure

"This is my last message to you: in sorrow,
seek happiness."

—*Fyodor Dostoyevsky, The Brothers Karamazov*

arly the following year (2009), Pat's health began to rapidly decline. She limped, fell more often, and had a difficult time standing up without help. She slept more and complained more frequently of pain. Her doctors continued to attribute this sudden change to her multiple sclerosis worsening.

The status quo was not working, so as her condition got worse, we looked for different doctors to try to find a solution to her health problems. But Pat's options were limited because she was on Medicaid, and as we learned quickly, most doctors do not treat Medicaid patients. Because of this, Pat had been visiting a clinic about an hour away that handled Medicaid patients. The doctors did not seem to stay at the clinic very long, so there was little continuity in treatment. It was probably very stressful for the doctors, and they were likely quite overworked. Pat had a good relationship with one doctor; then he left. The next doctor was hard to get appointments with, and when she did see her, Pat was frustrated that the doctor asked for more testing that did not seem relevant and did not address Pat's questions and concerns.

We desperately searched for new options. I called a large cancer center in the area, feeling confident they would see Pat and help her. We were very frustrated when they would not even see Pat because she was on Medicaid. Pat's healthcare options seemed to be running out. We all wanted magical answers, but we did not know where to go next. The current medical system was not working.

Aunt My, Ann's mother, recommended a local doctor, so we made an appointment and prayed he could help Pat. We called and asked if he took Medicaid, but there was an apparent misunderstanding. I recall that visit with Pat so clearly, as if it was yesterday. Pat and I arrived and entered the office waiting room. We were smiling, so happy to be together, and feeling very hopeful that Pat might have luck with a new doctor. We checked in and sat in the reception area waiting, talking and laughing, just knowing this doctor would help Pat.

The nurse asked for Pat's insurance card and saw it was Medicaid, then abruptly said, "Sorry, the doctor cannot see you. He does not accept Medicaid."

I asked if I could pay cash. They said no, they could not do that.

We begged them to let the doctor see her, but they just said, "No."

I recall standing there with Pat, both of us crying, desperately hugging each other. My stomach sank as the realization set in that Pat was running out of time.

That was my rude awakening to the American health-care system. It was horrible, and we were at our wit's end. No matter what we tried, we could not get Pat the help she needed. We could not get answers to what was going on with her.

In this fine country with the best of most everything — a country that brags about its healthcare and the finest, most expensive machines and medicine — we could not get my dear sister Pat good medical treatment.

Pat was being discarded as if she were a piece of garbage.

My sister was not a piece of garbage. She was a smart and beautiful woman with a loving heart who deserved so much better.

Another month passed, and spring arrived. Pat tried to carry on with her normal daily life. She planted her summer garden as she had done every year. She bought a few trays of annual flowers and two rose bushes, many of which she gave up planting, so I helped plant what she could not. One of Pat's favorite sections of Mom's garden was the front lawn, where she always planted multi-color annual flowers in the shape of a cross. Here she often prayed for help for Mom, herself and us all. Pat weeded and watered the plants every day as best she could to keep them thriving.

Another month went by and it was May, and there suddenly appeared a last glimmer of hope for Pat. I was listening to the radio and heard a presentation by a very interesting doctor. He impressed me with his knowledge of both conventional and alternative medicine. I felt sure he could help Pat, if anyone could. I called his office, discussed Pat's situation and healthcare, and made an appointment for later that month.

On the day of the appointment, I picked up Pat and Mom for our journey to the doctor. We drove over an hour on various highways and finally arrived at the doctor's office. This is another day I will never forget.

On arrival, a nurse gave Pat lengthy forms to complete with her medical history and family health history. As

Pat had lately had a difficult time seeing clearly, and the forms were long and too complicated for someone so ill to complete, I helped her fill them out. We were soon called in to meet with the doctor. Pat, Mom, and I were happy to meet him and very optimistic and excited that this doctor might be able to assist Pat. He asked what was wrong with her, and Pat explained her medical history, with assistance from Mom and me.

After spending about 10 minutes with the doctor, we found ourselves very impressed with his knowledge and caring disposition.

Suddenly, the doctor asked about Pat's insurance. When we told him Pat was on Medicaid, he froze up, apologized, and said there had been a misunderstanding — he was not able to treat her. He made some general recommendations, and we were quickly escorted out.

I think that was the turning point — the moment when my sister's hope of ever getting better ended. Pat seemed to lose her zest for life and the joyful sparkle in her eyes faded. All hope had died. Pat lost her desire to live.

Summer arrived. We all did the best we could, hoping for a good, happy summer, but that was not to be. It turned out these would be the last six months before Pat's death. They would be very difficult for everyone, but most of all for Pat.

CHAPTER 12

It's All Down Hill

"Everything constantly changes ... nothing stays the same and you have to adjust."

—Mom

*I*t was the morning of June 22nd, Joe's birthday, when Mom called frantically.

"Joanie, please come over now. I need help! It's an emergency!"

Pat could not stand up by herself all of a sudden, and could not walk to the bathroom. Our 91-year-old Mom was trying to help Pat walk and get her to the bathroom and into bed.

I rushed to Mom's house. I helped Mom assist Pat to the bathroom and into bed, but Pat was what you'd call dead weight. Though she only weighed about one hundred and thirty pounds, we had great difficulty lifting her.

Based on what the doctors had told us previously, it appeared Pat's multiple sclerosis had reached the tipping point. We needed help. And we needed help now. We talked with Pat and tried to decide what to do.

Pat desperately wanted to stay at home with Mom and her dogs, so we ordered a home hospital bed, then began interviewing home-care assistants later that day. Before we could retain a home-care assistant, Pat started having very painful headaches and began taking some painkillers that made her feel a bit more comfortable. Then all Pat wanted to do was to drink soda and take painkillers. It seemed the soda was making the headaches worse, but she insisted on drinking it. That was the only drink or food she craved, but when she drank it, her headaches got worse and worse, and she wanted more painkillers. Obviously, this was not good.

We quickly faced the sad realization that Pat needed good 24-hour care, with special medical and nursing care to help her and relieve her pain. Mom and I agreed Pat could not live with Mom in her condition, even with assistance. We just could not take care of her.

Pat's pain become unbearable, so Mom and I called 911 emergency for assistance, and an ambulance took Pat to the emergency room at the local hospital. We needed to know why Pat's condition declined so suddenly, and to see if there was something that could be done to help her.

I drove Mom to the hospital, and Joe met us there. Aunt Millie and Aunt Tillie, Mom's sisters from Perth Amboy, came to visit. We gathered around Pat and stayed with her, making sure she was comfortable, had nourishment and water, and was relaxed.

Pat was in the emergency room for hours, but it felt like an eternity. Many doctors came by to see her, and many tests were taken, including blood tests, CT scans, and so on. The doctors were very concerned about her and tried to get to the root of her problems.

Finally, one doctor came by to report.

"We have your diagnosis. It is not multiple sclerosis that is causing you these problems. It is brain cancer."

We were dumbfounded.

It appeared that all the diagnoses of multiple sclerosis recently were wrong, perhaps hastily made because Pat was on Medicaid. It was probably a logical conclusion that Pat's multiple sclerosis was getting worse. Unfortunately, none of the doctors had done additional testing to confirm if her deteriorating condition was truly because of multiple sclerosis, or if it was from another disease.

Pat was admitted for further testing and evaluation. We could not believe this was happening. One day it was multiple sclerosis, today brain cancer. Pat, understandably, had a very difficult time coming to terms with her condition. Brain cancer is a horrible diagnosis. A friend at my work had it and had all the operations and treatments that his doctors recommended. He returned to work for a couple of months after the treatment and looked healthy, then suddenly died.

Was our beloved dear Pat dying? This could not be happening. Pat had always been so vibrant, energetic, healthy, and strong. We started to question everything. How did this happen? Was it her diet or something else? Or was it everything together?

But all that did not matter now. We just did not want Pat to die. We were frantic and desperately wanted to cure her somehow. Naively, we hoped for a magical treatment that would reverse Pat's illness and make her healthy again. We did what we could. We asked for a healthy vegetarian diet for her. She could not smoke at the hospital, so that was good and surely would help. After a few days, Pat looked much better, had lots of color in her face and felt better — perhaps these minor changes gave her better circulation? Cousins Ann, Rich, and Janie believed Pat had not looked so good in years.

Surprisingly, Pat responded very well to the diet change, even to the point where the doctors noted how energetic she had become. They went so far as to recommend therapy and walking exercises for her.

That hope was short-lived. Pat seemed to improve, until the end of the week when the doctors terminated therapy because her improvement had plateaued. Pat was not making progress any longer.

Further tests were done, then a specialist called me aside.

"Your sister has very advanced brain cancer, and there is nothing more we can do for her."

Terminal cancer. They recommended putting Pat in a nursing home or hospice for her last days.

The doctors explained Pat's serious condition to her, and explained they could not operate or treat her with chemotherapy or radiation as the brain cancer was too far gone.

Nothing the doctors could do would help Pat.

The doctors further explained that the cancer was spreading, and eventually, it would grow and spread down toward her neck. There it would break a cord or something, causing her to die. This was hard for Pat and all of us to come to terms with. We could not imagine what she was going through — what it was like to know you were dying.

Pat stared at me and asked, "Why is this happening to me?"

I had no answer, and for a moment, I thought it would have been better if it was me this was happening to, not Pat. How could someone so wonderful be dying from this horrible disease at such a young age? Pat was only 58 years old, and had always lived life to the fullest. She was a good person all her life and tried to be nice to everyone and everything, though at times that was impossible to do because of her illnesses. She loved God and nature, and would even pet bumble bees and tell them how wonderful they were. She was a gentle soul. Why, oh, why was this happening? Our hearts went out to this beautiful girl.

∞

Pat was transferred to a local nursing home, the only one in the area with 24-hour doctor coverage. That was good because Pat would have a doctor on call any time of the day if she had severe pain or needed immediate assistance.

I became Pat's primary caregiver and visited her every day to check on her, to make sure she was doing as well as could be and had everything she needed. At first, I spent nearly the entire day with her, every day, to keep her company and try to help her get acclimatized to what life had just slammed her with.

Pat made friends quickly, getting along well with her roommate and becoming pals with many of her nurses and healthcare assistants. I felt comfortable leaving her and getting back to work, but visited her every day, some days before work, but always every night after work on my way home.

Every day when I returned home, exhausted from driving almost two hours on a good day to get to work, working all day, then driving another two hours to visit and care for Pat, Marly and Shaman were always there to greet me with smiling faces and tails wagging. They were such a joy in my life and helped fulfill my life and keep me sane.

I took Mom and George to visit Pat on weekends and other days off, sometimes with Bijou, which made Pat very happy. Joe, Ann, Rich, Irene, Sal, cousin Joe, RJ, Joe's brother Frank and his wife Donna, and other friends and relatives stopped by when they could.

One of the first things the nursing home requested of me was to designate Pat as a *Do Not Resuscitate* (DNR) patient. They told me this meant that if something happened to Pat, such as a heart attack, they would let her pass quickly rather than go through all the roughness of trying to resuscitate her.

Several family members who had worked in a number of hospitals in their lifetimes told me not to do that yet. They advised that, from their experience, the hospital staff would ignore Pat and not help her if she needed even the smallest bit of care. I discovered later that they were so right.

Pat had just entered the healthcare system, so I did not feel comfortable making her a DNR so quickly. Pat was still so energetic and clear-minded that I could not bring myself to even think of that. At first, and until her last weeks, I kept Pat as a full resuscitation patient, to the dismay of some.

I felt very responsible for Pat. She was my beloved older sister, my only sister, and my best friend. She was so helpless and vulnerable right now, she needed me to do my best to help her. As kids, Pat and I were very close, though there was an eight-year age difference between us. She adored me and called me her "Little Peepchu," with deep affection. Pat had always looked out for me and helped make sure I was okay. When Pat started working in New York City with Dad at Evyan Perfumes, she bought me a silver heart necklace, on which was engraved, "To Joan, Love Pat." I will treasure that — and you — forever, dear sister.

We had fun growing up and hanging out together, I looked up to Pat and learned so much from her. I was always thrilled when she took time out of her busy schedule to spend time with me, even if it was for a short walk in the neighborhood, playing Scrabble, Monopoly, or a card game, and of course to take a ride to the local pizzeria.

Best of all were our trips down to the New Jersey shore or to visit New York City, especially Rockefeller Center at Christmas time.

Now Pat was terminally ill and seemed so fragile compared to how strong and full of life she used to be. She needed me more than ever.

CHAPTER 13

Learning the Ropes

"When you think things have gotten as bad as they can be, you may get a surprise."

—Joni

When I looked at Mom, I saw the pain she was suffering from watching her oldest daughter suffer from cancer, dying slowly before her. I wished with my heart and soul I could do something to help Pat and make her better, so life could go back to the way it used to be.

Mom, Pat, and I had enjoyed so much fun together through the years, and together, we were a team of love. We had always gotten along well, trusting and helping each other. Just being together had given us a sense of joy and contentment; it did not take words to explain our relationship.

We had taken those happy days for granted, and now they were gone in the blink of an eye. Pat's illness was heartbreaking, and Mom was devastated. I did my best every day to fight for Pat so she would be cared for well and feel the best she could, given the circumstances, and so that Mom and all of us would get to spend more time with her. I believe in miracles and very much wished a miracle would happen so Pat would be cured.

I did a lot of research on cancer, multiple sclerosis, arthritis and the other diseases with which Pat was diagnosed. I read through websites and books on cancer, poring through Harvard Medical studies and other websites in the hopes of finding a cure. I researched conventional, holistic, and alternative care treatments and learned a lot about diet and supplements.

I put together a short presentation for the nursing home staff, suggesting where they could improve their diets for people with illnesses and the elderly to make them feel better and be healthier. Staff members were very nice and appreciative, but they pointed out to me that they really did the best they could with the limited funding and resources they have. They said there was nothing more they could do.

If they could not give Pat healthier foods, I would. I shopped for all kinds of organic vegetables, fruits, and vegetarian food. I made Pat homemade vegan pasta (she loved pasta and pizza!), and she looked forward to that each weekend when I visited.

In addition to healthier food, Mom and I made her room colorful and cheery with pretty wall hangings, and brought her many of her favorite stuffed animals from home. And we took her beloved furry friend Bijou to visit her, which made her smile cheek-to-cheek, so filled with joy.

All seemed to go well. Pat looked great and her attitude was good; I dared to hope she would not get any worse for a long time. Even if she had to stay in the nursing home for years, we would visit her every day. Perhaps selfishly, we just wanted Pat with us.

Pat reminded me in some ways of our Aunt Bertha, now deceased, who was immobile and confined to a nursing home for nearly 13 years due to severe rheumatoid arthritis. Though she was bedridden, she always had a big smile on her face, despite her worsening condition.

Family and friends visited Aunt Bertha every week, feeling so sad for her and bringing her gifts. But when we arrived and saw Aunt Bertha, it was like the sun coming out on a rainy day. She smiled and chatted with everyone, then she would start singing. She made each and every one of us feel so special and happy to be there with her, that she cheered us up! Then she would send us on our way with handmade gifts from her, made long ago, but most of all, we always left with a warm heart and big smiles on our faces because of the love she gave to us. She was truly an angel from heaven.

We hoped this would be the case for Pat — that her condition would remain stable and she would be happy in the nursing home for many years. Pat had good days, and not-so-good days, as the cancer advanced. Her spirits were usually very high, and much of the time, she loved chatting with everyone who visited, making us happy just as Aunt Bertha had done years ago.

Pat had funny, and sometimes sexy, stories that made me blush and the nurses laugh so hard they almost cried. The nurses loved to talk with Pat, and they enjoyed sharing funny stories and laughing together.

Pat especially enjoyed the visits from therapy dogs. How she missed her two dogs! Mom knew how much Bijou and Gibran meant to Pat, so she did her best to take good care of them, with the lingering hope that a miracle would happen and Pat would come home.

The boys were good companions for Mom, and having them by her side, it was as if Mom still had part of Pat at home with her. Mom took loving care of them, and in return, they followed her everywhere to keep an eye on her. They slept by her side when she watched television, and seemed to know she was older and were very gentle with her. They were very good watchdogs and barked at the smallest sound, helping Mom feel safe and secure.

Mom and I continued to take Bijou to visit Pat. She was always thrilled to see him and could not stop smiling and talking to him, hugging and scratching him. How she loved him! I could not imagine how sad it was for her not to be able to have her dogs with her.

I quickly noticed that many people at the nursing home were similarly situated. Some people had had pets all their lives but could no longer have any, so they greatly missed having them at their sides. And sadly, many residents never seemed to have any family or friends visit. Perhaps they did not have anyone left, or perhaps they lived far away and could not visit?

I began to deeply appreciate how important the work of nursing home activities staff is. They are truly angels, with a lot of responsibility as they try to keep everyone mentally and physically active and doing interesting activities so the residents can enjoy each day as best as they can.

As such, Pat, Mom, and I were thrilled when the activities team told us the nursing home was planning to have a fair outdoors in the courtyard. They announced there would be food, ice cream, popcorn, games with prizes, and best of all, there would be barnyard animals including cows, sheep, and chickens. How Pat loved farm animals!

We could not wait for the fair.

The day finally arrived, and Mom and I arrived early to see Pat. We spent the day at the fair with her, and all of us had a fun and memorable time. Pat loved it. We had such a good time it was hard to leave, but we finally took Pat back to her room and kissed her good night, and I took Mom home. It was to be one of the last happy days for Pat.

The next day, the nursing home called me to advise that Pat was being transferred from the nursing home to the hospital because she had contracted pneumonia. Mom and I could not believe it. Pat looked so good yesterday, energetic, healthy, and happy, and now she had congestion and difficulty breathing.

Joe and I rushed to the hospital to find Pat had been admitted to a room and was having antibiotics administered. She was awake and in good spirits, so we stayed with her until after she ate, settled in and went to sleep. She was in very good hands, we believed. The nursing home advised that Pat might be in the hospital for some time, so we transferred her belongings to the hospital.

I saw Pat daily to spend time with her and check her condition. We all hoped she would get rid of the pneumonia and feel well enough soon to return to the nursing home. Needless to say, this new challenge to Pat's health had Mom feeling very worried.

CHAPTER 14

Catching It All

"Don't ever give up on someone you love."

—Joni

*P*at enjoyed spending hour after hour with us when we visited her in the hospital. She never wanted us to leave, although she was exhausted from the pneumonia and slept a lot. We hoped her pneumonia would be cured quickly.

The doctors kept trying new medications and other treatments, but nothing was working. Pat was in the hospital one day, then two days, then a week. Her condition was not improving.

Then to our horror, Pat started contracting other diseases. We were told her immune system was compromised, making it easier for her to catch other diseases from the germs in the hospital.

Although I always wanted to see Pat, I became apprehensive about going to the hospital. It seemed almost every day when I arrived, a doctor or nurse was chasing me down to tell me Pat had a new disease. I felt as though there was a lookout who notified the doctor on duty I was there. It amazed all of us that a doctor or nurse would enter Pat's room a few minutes after my arrival to share the news of Pat's next disease.

It seemed unbelievable that Pat could contract so many diseases, but it was true.

"We are sorry, Pat came down with herpes today," I was told.

"We are so sorry, Pat has contracted MRSA," I was then advised.

MRSA? That's usually deadly, isn't it? I have heard many sad stories from friends whose family members went into the hospital for a "simple" operation, then contracted pneumonia or MRSA. Then bang! They were dead a couple of weeks later. How could this be happening to Pat?

Appallingly, this continued. The next time I visited, I discovered Pat now had a tough time swallowing because she had developed a rash in her throat, and it was very sore. She could no longer eat her favorite foods like pizza and hamburgers because they were too acidic; it just hurt too much.

Then Pat contracted edema. Her entire body swelled up, especially her legs and arms. To our astonishment, they swelled up to nearly twice their normal size.

Pat's albumin was low, the doctor said. Then Pat became anemic, then it was dehydration, followed by malnutrition. Pat was catching everything the hospital germs had to offer!

The next thing the doctor told me was that Pat had contracted something called C-diff, but, "Do not worry, they are treating everything as best they can."

To my horror, the doctors and nurses went from telling me Pat had a new disease, to telling me that *because* Pat had a new disease, I should change her status to *Do Not Resuscitate*.

Just when I believed Pat's condition could not get any worse, it did.

Early one morning I received a call — the doctor was transferring Pat to the Intensive Care Unit (ICU). Pat was now in a coma and had a rapidly rising fever.

How could this be happening?

Mom and I visited Pat in ICU, praying she would somehow get better. We did everything we could think of to communicate with her and encourage her not to give up. Though Pat was in a coma, I just knew somehow she could hear us, so we spoke to her with love and inspiration to let her know she would be okay.

I brought a compact-disc player and played some of Pat's favorite music, hoping she would hear it and be cheered up, then wake up. Her favorite songs lit up the ICU. We played best hits and love songs by Marlene Dietrich, Marilyn Monroe, and Johnny Mathis, The Nutcracker Suite, Charlie Brown's Christmas (Pat's favorite holiday), and other timeless music. We sat with Pat for hours, talking to her, singing, massaging her swollen arms and legs, and praying.

One day, the head doctor in charge of the ICU unit (I called him the "God of ICU") came into Pat's room and said to me, in Pat's presence, "Look at her."

I did.

He proceeded to talk about Pat's condition, and told me we should put her in hospice.

Pat was still in a coma and had well over a dozen intravenous drips attached to her, containing antibiotics and other drugs, liquids, and nutrition to sustain her. She had an oxygen mask on her face attached to a mechanical ventilator to assist her with breathing.

My sister seemed to be dying prematurely from all the diseases she had contracted while in the hospital, not from the cancer.

"Yes, Doctor, I see how poorly Pat is doing," I thought. Then I cringed, because I was sure Pat could hear what he had said about her condition. I told the doctor I would not give up on my dear sister.

With a sinking feeling in my heart, I called William to tell him it did not look good for Pat, and that he should come out and see her for what may be the last time. William drove from Pittsburgh that night.

I went home and hugged Marly and Shaman.

William is the oldest of Mom's children. Her pride and joy, he has a big loving heart, total devotion to our family, and is very religious. He is also very smart and a wonderful conversationalist, which helped him to be a very successful salesman in his career. Like Pat, he can hold a good conversation with anyone.

It was heartwarming for my Mom and me to have William with us. We were all together again. He gave us additional much-needed support at this difficult time, although we did not know yet if his purpose was to help Pat or to say a final goodbye.

CHAPTER 15

The Miracle

"Miracles do happen."

—Joni

*W*illiam and I could see the heartbreak on Mom's face and the toll Pat's illness was taking on her. As Pat's prime caregiver, I felt I just had to do something. I understood what the doctors said, but I could not let Pat die like this right now. Not now, not from all the diseases unrelated to her cancer. For Mom's sake.

When Pat first arrived in ICU, her temperature was low but rising. It was now approaching 105 degrees and climbing. I had to try something fast.

I did more research ... lots of research, about the diseases Pat had.

MRSA, pneumonia, edema, herpes, fever, and cancer.

Conventional cures. Alternative medicine cures. Holistic natural cures. Dietary cures.

I had no idea if any of my research would help Pat, but I did know this — the treatments the doctors were administering were *not working*. Pat's condition was getting worse every day. It was clear that somehow we needed to come up with Plan B.

I had found certain natural cures on the Internet that I thought might help cure Pat of some of the diseases she had contracted in the hospital. Some of the articles I read suggested that many of her diseases may have been contracted because of a compromised immune system, and many of them could be related.

Certain foods and garden herbs kept appearing over and over in Internet search results and research articles as being possible natural cures for pneumonia, MRSA, and some of her other diseases. My instinct told me there must be some truth to all of this.

I mentioned some of these natural cures to the God of ICU and asked for his opinion. He responded by saying pretty much that all of what I had researched was, "hogwash nonsense." He said none of it would work.

I told this to my brother as tears rolled down my face. My brother, seeing how upset I was, approached the doctor.

"Doctor, if you do not think Pat is going to live, then why do you care if we give her something? Let us try these, they are natural foods and cannot hurt her."

To our surprise, the God of ICU said, "Okay, fine, tell me what you want to do and how much and I will prescribe it."

I could not believe my ears.

"Thank you, Doctor!" I quickly replied.

I came up with a rational ratio, and the now elevated-to-wonderful doctor wrote out an order to do what I asked, starting the next morning. I had some hope, and went home to get some sleep, where I was eagerly welcomed by Marly and Shaman and covered with kisses.

To my surprise, I returned the next day to find the nurses had started administering my recipe to Pat through the intravenous tubes — with joy I must add, as they were quite excited about it.

Mom and I prayed these foods would help make a difference.

We sat with Pat for hours, holding her hand, massaging her arms and legs, and speaking to her. Although I knew some of the hospital staff probably thought we were a bit crazy, we played more happy music and love songs for Pat and sang along.

"Playing this music may not work," I thought, "but it sure did liven up the ICU, and cheer up many of the doctors, nurses, aides, and I would bet some of the patients."

Most of all, I hoped all our efforts would help Pat. It just had to work. The wonderful nurses administered the blend to Pat twice each day.

Returning together the next day, Mom and I were astonished! To our joy and amazement, Pat's fever had declined significantly, as had the swelling of her arms and legs from the edema. Her body appeared to be quickly returning to normal!

Mom and I talked to Pat, telling her how good she was doing, and that she was improving quickly. Then Mom started asking Pat to wake up.

"Pat, please wake up. It's Mom! We love you!"

Mom and I had tears of joy when Pat suddenly moved a bit and slowly opened her eyes. She recognized us immediately, and though it was difficult at first, she began to speak to us. It was magical.

To our amazement, Pat continued to improve daily and was discharged from ICU by the end of the week — less than a week after starting to get the natural foods in the IV, she was transferred back to a regular hospital room.

All of us were ecstatic. One of Pat's doctors, a very nice man, came up to me, smiling elatedly and said, "It is a miracle! It is a miracle!"

Alternatively, the brain surgeon who had confirmed Pat's brain cancer, and drilled into her head to biopsy brain cells while she was in the coma, had different words.

I was driving to work one morning when he called my cell phone and very untastefully said to me, "I hear your sister is out of ICU — I thought she was dead."

I was lost for words. A few days later, Mom received a get-well card for Pat from him. He probably realized how horrible the statement he had made to me about Pat was.

∞

About that time, our beloved Belgian Tervuren, Marly, now thirteen years old and graying, suddenly developed a reduced appetite.

We took him to our vet, who referred us to a specialist. Marly had stomach cancer, a disease too common to many dog breeds nowadays, and there was nothing they could do. The specialist said Marly was not in pain but was in good spirits.

I was broken-hearted, and wondered if Marly became ill because of what was happening around him. Marly surely sensed the high stress and deep sadness we all felt because Pat was very sick. Although Joe was caring for the boys, they must have missed me, because I left early in the morning some days to visit Pat before work, and most nights I went right to the hospital or nursing home to visit Pat after work. Often I did not get home until late, not to mention the emergency calls in the middle of the night.

Our stress certainly takes a toll on dogs, who are so in tune with us, our emotions, and well-being. We gave Marly extra love and the best food and supplements so he would continue to eat, and did the best we could for him while praying for the best. He seemed to stabilize for a while and hung in there. When it rains it pours, does it not?

CHAPTER 16

Pat's Decline

*"Sometimes all you can do is be with your loved one
and give them all the love and compassion you have."*

—Joni

Shortly after Pat's release from ICU to a regular hospital room, the doctor in charge wanted to transfer Pat back to the nursing home. I hesitated because Pat was still very weak. I asked the doctor if Pat would receive the same medical care as in the hospital. She assured me she would.

I was promised Pat would get all the same care — including hydration, because Pat could not drink enough water, additional nutrition because sometimes her appetite was not good, and a leg massage machine that would help prevent blood clots, as Pat could no longer move her legs. Based on that promise, late one day Pat was transferred back to the nursing home.

When I visited the nursing home early the next morning, to my shock, Pat was already hallucinating. She was very dehydrated, clearly the main cause of this, having had no water or nutrition, and she was in a lot of pain.

Pat did not get what was promised her.

Horrified, my family and I thought this was malpractice and mentioned our concern to her rotating doctor and staff. It was a coincidence perhaps, but Pat received much better treatment after we mentioned the 'M' word. Pat was immediately transferred back to the hospital into a first-class private room with a refrigerator, a visitor couch that converted to a bed, and other nice furniture, not that Pat could appreciate any of it in her condition. I think they were only trying to appease me.

Again, staff were clearly told to notify the social worker, nurse, or doctor when I arrived at the hospital. I was confronted within minutes of my arrival every visit.

Family chats formerly had been limited to formal meetings with all staff. But now the administration aggressively sought my agreement to put Pat on DNR. I fully understood why, but this really was not my decision.

Although I was Pat's primary caregiver, I believed it was Pat's decision, and her mind was still clear enough most of the time to decide what she wanted to have happen to her. If Pat was not able to make that decision at some point, at the least, it was a family decision, something for all of us to discuss, not just for me to decide alone. We were all in this together. We are family.

Unfortunately, although Pat's other illnesses had seemed to disappear, her brain cancer had progressed. She could not see clearly and started hallucinating at times, sometimes seeing imaginary insects on the ceiling. As we were warned would happen, she sometimes saw people who were not visible to the rest of us. This was all in the pamphlet the nursing home had given Mom and me that warned about what can happen before someone dies.

As part of her hallucinations, Pat imagined she had a baby and that Mom took it away from her. She wanted the baby back. I learned quickly that to keep her calm and content, I needed to play along or she would get very upset, which did not help her — or anyone, so I strongly assured Pat that I would help get her baby back.

Pat also began to see people who were long deceased. She thought Dad was still alive and asked about him. She saw old friends and their parents and would start talking with them. I played along as best as I could. I knew if I did not, Pat would become confused, then very upset. I made that mistake once and learned from it. And besides, who was I to say who Pat was now able to see and not see?

It was about keeping Pat happy, not about correcting her because she said something I thought might be incorrect. It was about keeping her in as stable a condition emotionally and physically as we could, and if possible, to keep her happy and smiling. Pat did not have much time left, so the doctors and nurses said. And a lesson I learned from this, though I wish I had learned it at a happier time, is that none of us may have a lot of time left, so we should be nice to each other and to all other beings all of the time.

We had addressed most of Pat's health problems, but could not cure her brain cancer. Her condition slowly worsened as the cancer grew, with the headaches growing steadily more severe. Her eyesight continued to worsen, and sometimes her eyes hurt because the cancer was building up pressure within her head. The doctors transitioned Pat from Tylenol to Percocet and Fentanyl patches (opioids) to address the ever-increasing pain she felt in her head, and when the pain became unbearable, to morphine drops in her mouth. How Pat hated morphine and the nausea that followed.

Unfortunately, sometimes the nurses were so busy that it took a long time for them to give Pat the painkillers. Often when that happened, the pain became so intolerable that Pat screamed until the painkillers started taking effect.

Her appetite decreased, and she had a permanent feeding tube inserted into her stomach to make up for the decline in nutrients. Pat still ate and drank, but not often enough in quantities that would keep her properly nourished and hydrated without the tube.

On a bad day, Pat had several hallucinations and sometimes would say she wished she could go home and die. But most days, she would somehow still have a very positive attitude. She would say in a determined way that she would beat this. She so much wanted to get better and go home to live with Mom. As such, no one could make the decision to let her go yet.

We had many good days together toward the end. Pat's mind was still clear, and she always knew who we were. She remembered so many good times and funny stories we shared together. Some of my best memories of that time were of us joking and laughing with Mom and singing Christmas songs and Pat's favorite fun tunes, like *La Cucaracha*.

All of us were joyful to spend happy, quality times together for almost four more months after Pat was released from ICU. We visited, talked, joked around, and had fun with her. We smiled, reminisced, and laughed, we talked about her dogs and how they could not wait until she returned home. And this gave us a little more time to adjust to the fact that Pat was indeed dying.

We talked about her upcoming birthday on December 27, and how the number "27" was her favorite lucky number. Mom and I hoped to celebrate her birthday with her and told Pat's favorite nurses about the upcoming special day. Everyone looked forward to that day.

The big birthday celebration was not to be. A couple of weeks into December, Pat became tired more of the time and slept more, and oddly, she said she started to feel less pain. Before we knew it, it was December 20th, seven days before Pat's 59th birthday. The weather news predicted a massive snowstorm to start that afternoon. Pat had loved snow, for as long as I could recall. Years ago, she would call me, Mom, and the rest of the family at the first sighting of a snowflake.

Thus, it was quite fitting that Pat would pass on and make her grand departure from this world during one of the worst snowstorms of 2009. She was only 58 years old.

CHAPTER 17

The Storm

"When you are deeply saddened over the loss of a loved one, remember that you are sad because that very special someone brought you much joy. Treasure the good times that you had with them and feel blessed they were a miracle in your life."

—Joni

Joe and I visited Pat that morning, ahead of the storm. Pat was sleeping, but her breathing was a bit heavier than normal, as if a cold was coming on. I asked the nurse to notify the doctor of this, which she promptly did. The doctor promised to check on her shortly.

We stayed for a while longer, but left because the storm was strengthening very quickly. We could see from Pat's window that the roads were rapidly getting snow-covered. We made it home safely just before the storm transitioned into a massive blizzard. How it snowed! In the old days, Pat would have loved to watch this.

I called Mom to let her know how Pat was doing. Evening came quickly; we all said prayers for Pat, then tried to get some sleep. The storm continued.

Early the next morning, I received a call that Pat was being shuttled back to the hospital for observation. I assured myself this was good because Pat would have the full hospital team looking after her and treating her.

Hours later, I received another call from the doctor advising they'd done a CT scan of Pat's brain. The news was dreadful — the test confirmed Pat's brain cancer had grown and that was what was affecting her breathing ability. The situation was irreversible, and treatment would not help.

The doctor put Pat on a breathing machine to help her breathe, but she was starting to fail. Her blood pressure was decreasing. I needed to pick up Mom and get to the hospital right away. Mom wanted to see Pat, her oldest daughter, before she passed.

I looked outside. The snow had stopped, but it had accumulated at least two feet. The roads were not yet plowed by the town, so there was no way I could drive through this snow.

Joe plowed our long driveway as fast as he could, and soon the town arrived to plow the streets. While Joe went inside to warm up, the town accidentally plowed us back in again, leaving a big wall of snow in front of our driveway. Joe plowed us out again, and I left immediately for Mom's house, driving on the slick, partially plowed roads.

I finally reached Mom's, shoveled her driveway and walkway and helped her to my car. We hurried to the hospital to see Pat one last time, with me driving as carefully as I could on the slippery roads.

We were too late. Less than an hour before, Pat had passed on to her next phase of being. We were devastated. We knew this was coming but it was so difficult to accept.

We kissed Pat and held her hands, which were now getting cold. Then Mom started talking to Pat, and my heart broke in two.

"Patty, wake up! Patty, it is Mom. Please wake up. Do it for me."

Mom held back her tears and tried to smile, praying with her heart and soul that Pat would wake up like all the other times she'd awakened up from a deep sleep at home and at the ICU. But Pat had moved on. Mom and I started to cry, hugging each other.

Pat was really gone.

Joe arrived at the hospital soon after us. I phoned my cousin Ann, and she and Rich came by. We stayed with Pat at the hospital for a long time. Although we knew how sick Pat had been, none of us could believe this dear, beloved beautiful woman, once so full of life, strength, and energy, and such a large part of our lives, was no longer with us.

Suddenly, the sun came out. With all the fresh clean snow, it was so bright outside. The snow sparkled like a mound of brilliant diamonds.

Though the day was bitter cold, and now very empty with Pat's passing, there was something overwhelmingly beautiful about the snow, the ice-covered glistening trees, the brightly shining sun, and the colorful cardinals and blue jays we saw outside that reminded me of Pat's love for nature. I could feel Pat's warm presence in my heart and knew she was with us.

Pat, with her great love of snow and huge snow storms, made her grand exit from this Earth as the storm ended. It was not difficult to believe that Pat had arranged for this nor'easter as her magnificent farewell celebration. She knew how to throw a splendid party and could not have had a more perfect send-off. It was so fitting.

Surely, she was now in her heaven, having fun and busily making new friends and hugging old ones. We believed she paused for a moment to look down upon us, smiling her joyful, loving smile. She was free and happy again, no longer in pain.

∞

Later that day, I saw one of Pat's doctors and asked her what Pat had actually died from. I needed closure. She told me it was the brain cancer that progressed and pushed part of her brain down towards her neck and cut off or broke something there, as they predicted.

I asked if Pat still had pneumonia when she passed.

No.

Herpes?

No.

MRSA?

No.

Anything else?

No.

"It was only the cancer that was left," the doctor said.

Odd, Pat's death certificate says she passed from metastatic lung cancer. X-rays from one test showed something they had suspected was lung cancer, but they told me they had reversed this opinion after later testing.

Pat's funeral was a few days later. Pat had always loved parties — she was the master of planning them in her younger days. She loved celebrations for birthdays and holidays, and her favorite holiday was Christmas, so we presented her with a grand farewell party by having a celebration of her life with her favorite people and many of her favorite things, a sendoff she surely loved.

We ordered Pat a beautiful white casket and lovely flowers. Because she loved Christmas so much, we decorated a Christmas tree next to her coffin with lots of bright white lights and purple and white Christmas balls, purple being her favorite color. I placed her favorite stuffed snowman I had given her for Christmas years before in front of her coffin, along with 27 festive red poinsettia plants that we placed on the floor around her (27 was Pat's favorite number). Magnificent flowers from family, friends, and coworkers surrounded her.

On display were photos of Pat with the family and her dogs, and her paintings. There was no room for sad music, instead, her favorite joyful music brightened up the funeral parlor. The gentleman working at the funeral home and taking care of the set-up was so nice, he gladly played this music for Pat. Judy Garland's *Easter Parade*, Frank Sinatra's love songs, and Charlie Brown's Christmas music cheered up the funeral home and helped us celebrate Pat's life. It was as perfect as a funeral could be.

Aunt Millie and Aunt Tillie said it was the happiest funeral they had ever been to. The happiest of funerals for a wonderful girl who stole our hearts. We were all very sad, but knew Pat was smiling down on us. It truly was a magnificent send-off.

CHAPTER 18

Learning Pains

"Only people who are capable of loving strongly can also suffer great sorrow, but this same necessity of loving serves to counteract their grief and heals them."

—*Leo Tolstoy*

I learned a lot from Pat's long illness and the research I had done. I often asked the doctors what could have caused Pat's cancer, but no one had any answers. After all my research, I didn't, either.

I had read that some diseases may be hereditary, also that something can cause a body's cells to mutate into cancer cells. Some research said that all of us have cancer cells within us, but for many people, something makes the cancer cells grow and thrive to the point that they can kill us.

Other research suggested that clean cells in the body become impacted or "get dirty" by certain bad substances entering the body. I read there can be many things that affect a cell's health and can cause cancer.

Unhealthy substances can enter our bodies via the water we drink, shower, or swim in, the food we eat, and the air we breathe. They can be hazardous substances and other pollution, chemicals in our food, cookware, items we touch or wear, the airwaves, and from electronics and radiation. I read that stress, lack of sleep, and not enough oxygen and exercise are among the many other things that can cause an imbalance in a body's system and enable disease to occur.

I read if a person is healthy and strong enough, their body sometimes naturally fights off those things and any cell mutations they cause, and off they go, healthy for a while. Sometimes we can counteract an imbalance and sometimes we cannot, and it won't matter what we do.

Some people may be more susceptible or predisposed to certain illnesses. Two people can be in the same place, and one can come down with an illness and the other not, such as in the instance of exposure to or contact with hazardous substances.

And that is why I struggled with Pat's illnesses. Some seemed to be curable with a mix of conventional medicines plus some holistic methods. Some cancers are more treatable than others and that gives people hope. But for Pat's brain cancer, the doctors told us there were no treatments and no cures.

Pat's cancer had been misdiagnosed for so long, and by the time it was properly diagnosed was too far advanced to combat. We also wondered if Pat's pain would have been more manageable, and without unpleasant side effects, with cannabidiol (CBD) oil and the medical marijuana treatments that are becoming legal and very popular now.

All in all, despite the billions of dollars spent on cancer research, racing for cures, and the never-ending war on cancer that started many decades ago, there was not one thing the doctors could do to help Pat. We have come a long way in some instances, and many people have been helped. Some of my friends have had conventional treatments and are cancer survivors, though they say the treatment was hideous, and with so many side effects, that they do not know if they would ever do it again if the cancer returned.

Sadly, most of my family and dear friends who have had cancer have died, despite faithfully going through the chemotherapy, radiation, and/or surgery protocols. They suffered so much with the cancer, and in some cases, more so from the treatment that did not save them. And recently, a very dear friend had an odd coincidental heart attack and died soon after taking a new cancer drug.

There is so much about cancer we do not know, but the questions I keep asking myself are: Finding cures is wonderful (and we should continue to do this and do a better job of it), *but why can we not find ways to spend as much money on the research, education, and active measures related to preventing cancers*? And why does the current healthcare system frown so much on alternative or complementary natural cures that can help cure people from many illnesses or in other ways?

Someone told me once that when something is not clear, do your homework and simply follow the money. Maybe we just need to follow the money and see who profits from all the chemicals and pollution in our food and environment, cancer treatments and related research, and the current healthcare system, to understand this more fully.

There clearly is not enough profit in cancer prevention or in natural cures yet. And it can be impossible to get someone to understand and support something new and different when that person's income source is fed from a very profitable but close-minded industry.

I had hoped Pat would get better for Mom's sake, and of course all of ours, but at some point during Pat's illness, other questions faced me. Were we trying to extend Pat's life, even though she was very sick and suffering, for our own selfish purposes, just so she could be with us a little longer? Or was it for her benefit, because it would really help her move forward with some more good time on this planet?

The answers seemed clear to some of the doctors, I imagine because they see so many people every day and probably know what is going to happen for the different diagnoses, so they try to move everyone along quickly as best they can.

But family members do not want to lose their beloved ones and do not see it that way, and they are faced with a dilemma in decision-making. It is a tough dilemma that we all may be faced with, sometimes many times.

Bottom line, unless some new technology arises, we all will die someday. No one is getting out of here alive, but as Joe says, he does not want to get sick and suffer from these horrible diseases. Somehow, he wants to die healthy, maybe in his sleep one day, but not prematurely. Yes, wouldn't we all?

But that may not happen, so perhaps we can help make our end-of-life decisions easier for our family and friends by making sure we set forth in the appropriate legal documents our desires and last wishes if we become terminally ill, so they do not have to carry all of that weight. We should also name appropriate trustees, and provide for the care of our furry and feathered friends so they are well taken care of after we depart.

CHAPTER 19

Missing Pat

*"We have less time than we think on this earth —
so live life to the fullest and be nice to everyone that
you meet."*

—*Joni*

Mom's heart broke in many pieces after Pat passed. She could only take so much grief. At some point, she developed a small bump on her neck. Her doctor wanted her to see a specialist, but she refused. She said she felt fine, her appetite and sleep were good, so she refused to go. Mom got very upset when we asked her to go to a specialist and have it checked out.

Despite Mom's protests, I made several doctor appointments for a checkup, but Mom cancelled the appointments, feisty as always. If we persisted, we knew she would get upset and start to cry. Rather than upset her further, with her frail heart (having been through a stroke and a quadruple bypass eight or so years before) we gave in to her wishes.

Mom would rather stay home and watch a Yankee game than go to the doctor for more bad news, so we moved on with life and tried to enjoy it to the fullest, knowing that our lives are so very fragile and short. We visited friends and relatives, shared good food, and laughed as often as we could.

One of our biggest, heartiest laughs came right before Halloween, one of Pat's favorite holidays. I drove Mom past a house in the Milton Lake section of her neighborhood. Whoever owned the house had done an amazing job decorating their front lawn outside with all kinds of scary figures on the lawn and roof, fake coffins on the ground, huge spiders in the trees, and scary sounds. It was a very special moment with Mom. We laughed so hard we cried tears of joy. We both thought of Pat and how she had decorated Mom's house in a similar way over 40 years before.

Pat was very creative and artsy, way ahead of her time. Not until the last decade or so did decorations of her caliber come out in the stores. Back in the 1960s, she drew and created Halloween and Christmas decorations, decorating Mom's house inside and out like a Halloween haunted house and Christmas city, throwing parties with music befitting of both occasions and costumes to fit. For Halloween, in addition to the decorations, Pat played spooky music both inside and outside of Mom's house, to Mom's horror. Then Pat invited friends and family over for a haunted house tour, followed by a costume party.

Later that day, I came across an appropriate anonymous quote, "We think we have more time than we really do." How true, as Pat's short life showed us. We never know when our time will come. Along with that came the realization that we should not waste a moment, and should enjoy the good things life has to offer. And, as many people say, be nice to everyone, including animals and all of nature along the way, and make this a kinder, gentler, and better place. We just never know who we will meet later on.

Months after Pat passed away, Mom asked me to help her go through Pat's personal belongings and clean out her room. Mom had put this off for quite a while, and I did not want to raise the sensitive subject. We gently and carefully went through Pat's items one by one, sharing our fond memories about each piece. We donated some of Pat's clothes and struggled with the rest. It hurt both of us emotionally, most of all because it hammered into us the realization that Pat was indeed gone.

Pat's cards, paintings, photos, and collectibles brought back many sweet memories. Then her diaries, letters, medical bills, prescriptions, and pills reminded us of many painful times during her illness. Mom and I found ourselves reliving Pat's illnesses and death, regretting not being at Pat's side when she passed away. Recalling Pat's last day and the months that led up to it were agonizing.

All of this reminded me of the diary I had started keeping when Pat's health took a sudden downturn just before she was admitted to the hospital. I had written down nearly everything I heard and saw during Pat's last months, probably because it was too much for me to take in and come to terms with at the time, and sometimes, frankly, I did not know what else to do.

I was not ready then to go back and look at the diary, knowing it would unleash so many painful emotions I had locked away. I did not open and read the diary again until recently, while writing this book.

CHAPTER 20

Mom and Bijou

"Time continues on, stopping for no one, no reason."

—Joni

*I*t is said that time waits for no one. Indeed, our lives went on, but life without Pat left a big void. Mom and I missed her greatly. Pat had always been such a happy, friendly gal with big smiles and a vibrant personality that I wish I had a lot more of. She was smart, and her mind worked very quickly. She always seemed a step ahead of everyone.

Pat was also a wonderful communicator. She could easily hold a conversation with anyone she met, and she had friends everywhere. In this day and age, where society has grown much colder, and full of hatred and mistrust, some people took her friendliness as odd, but the world would be a better place if there were more people like Pat.

Although Mom was devastated at the passing of Pat, losing a child being one of the toughest things that can happen to a parent, she kept her chin up and had very good spirits. She remained the strong matriarch of our family, and we and other family and friends frequently gathered together around her to continue in the celebration of birthdays and holidays, and simply to be together.

Mom was very tough behind her beautiful face. She had learned a lot about love, courage, and resiliency in her 90-plus years. One of eight daughters of Polish immigrants, Mom worked as a Rosie the Riveter during World War II, then married and raised three strong-willed children.

Mom remained a very elegant lady. We often told her she looked like a Hollywood star, always dressed in a stylish, colorful dress or pantsuit, with jewelry to match, and her favorite warm pink lipstick. Her naturally pale blonde/white shoulder-length hair was kept carefully styled in the hairstyles of the stars of the romantic '40s and '50s, teamed with her pretty, white-framed movie-star sunglasses. Mom continued to take life in her stride.

Without Pat, Mom now lived alone, but that was how she wanted it. She wanted to stay in her house and not burden family or friends, nor go to a nursing home. She loved her house where she had lived since she married Dad more than 50 years previously. She was independent and clear-minded, and very capable to be on her own with minimal assistance.

I visited Mom weekly and more, depending on what Mom needed. I shopped and did errands, trying my best to fill Pat's shoes, taking Mom with me whenever she wanted to go. We visited family and friends and went to her doctor visits. Though in her nineties, she still walked well, though sometimes with the assistance of a cane.

Eventually I got Mom a wheelchair for those long walks down the hallway to the doctors' offices. She was still very active at home, going up and down stairs despite our pleas not to, washing clothes, cooking, and making me healthy salads that we would eat together for lunch.

Mom loved her garden and nature. She believed everyone should get at least 15 minutes of sun every day, so she
would sit in her yard with Gibran and Bijou on a nice day
and rest there in the sun for a while, saying she needed
to take in some sunshine and Vitamin D. Her complexion
was healthy and glowing, too.

∞

Mom cared for Pat's two dogs, Gibran and Bijou, for as
long as she could. She enjoyed their company and protection and treasured them because Pat had loved them
so. But taking care of two dogs who liked to go outside
to potty in the middle of the night became difficult for
Mom, who was then 92 years old.

My brother's friends in Pennsylvania took in little
Gibran. It took some adjusting, but they became a happy
family.

I loved Bijou, and told Joe we were taking him in. I
had to do it for Pat. She would have wanted him to be
with me because she said the only people he loved and
trusted were her, Mom, and me. Bijou was very shy, having spent most of his life at Pat's feet during her illnesses,
and not getting out much other than going for walks or
rides when we visited.

One day, while my brother William was visiting from
Pittsburgh, he and Mom brought Bijou to our house to
meet Shaman and Rio. Shaman had just adjusted to Rio
moving in and was not thrilled to have another surprise
invader, no matter how nice, and no matter how shy. Rio,
alternatively, was ecstatic to have a new friend to play
with. Quickly, all the dogs became friends, and things
fell into place. Life was good once again.

Bijou was happy to be with us and have a large
fenced-in yard to run in, as well as some really good
home-cooked food. But though he knew and loved us,

emotionally he was going through a difficult time, being separated from his beloved Pat and his buddy Gibran. On top of that, he had to adjust to a new home and a much noisier and busier life.

Bijou was now eight years old. His life with Pat and Mom had been very quiet, and on most days, they were the only people he interacted with. Although it was difficult for Bijou to adjust to a new home, new owners, and new friends, very large changes all at once, it appeared to be the best option. We played, went for walks and rides, and had a lot of fun, and while Pat was in the nursing home, he had visited. Mom was so thrilled that he fit into our family so well. Sadly, our happy time with Bijou lasted less than a year.

One day, Bijou started losing his appetite, strange for the big, healthy Australian Shepherd who usually devoured his food. I felt over his body and found some small lumps on his neck. I took him to the vet immediately and he was diagnosed with lymphoma, a type of cancer.

His immune system was compromised, but the vet said there was hope, so I took Bijou to a cancer specialist. The specialist was kind and very caring, and explained that lymphoma is a type of cancer that is very treatable in dogs. She said they had a protocol of different drugs they would administer over several months, and nearly all dogs, all but about one percent, would go into remission and possibly live many years afterwards.

I was very hopeful. I loved Bijou, and he was one last living link to Pat, so I desperately wanted to take care of him for her and Mom and get him better, no matter what. I signed on for the treatment and faithfully took Bijou to the vet every other week.

We went for chemo treatment after chemo treatment. Each made Bijou sick for days, but then he responded quickly with a voracious appetite. We went to our last appointment hoping the lymphoma was going into remission.

To our surprise and deep sorrow, the vet told me, "I am so very sorry, but the chemo isn't working for Bijou, and there is nothing more we can do. He is one of the unlucky ones. It is just a matter of time. But the good news is he is not in any pain and will not be during this process."

No, this could not be happening. I cried at the thought of losing him, too.

The weeks went by, and Bijou's appetite slowly decreased. Bijou's spirits were still very good, he still ran around with Rio and Shaman in our yard, and hung out with us. He drank plenty of water, but he did not always eat all of his meals.

It was going to be very tough to lose Bijou, Pat's beloved buddy. Having him by my side was kind of like still having a part of Pat nearby. We made the best of each day and enjoyed every moment together, right up to the end.

I could never tell Mom her beloved Bijou had lymphoma and the available treatments didn't work. That would destroy her emotionally losing her and Pat's dear boy.

CHAPTER 21

Mom's Turn

*"Everything is not always as it seems to be, please do
research and ask questions."*

—Joni

In between my juggling act of working, helping Mom, and trying to maintain our house while Joe was away, I focused the little free time I had left on conformation classes with Rio and showing him in the conformation ring. Though we were not winning any points, I continued showing Rio. The show world was a much-needed distraction for me, bringing me many moments of happiness.

Then on an early summer day, I went to Mom's and something was not right. She needed help to get to the bathroom, but we did not get there quickly enough. Mom had diarrhea on the hallway rug and bathroom floor. It was an abnormal black color.

I was frightened.

Mom said she felt okay, but I knew something was not right, so I made an appointment immediately with her doctor and asked William to come out from Pennsylvania to help, and thank goodness he did. We saw Mom's doctor, and he sent us to a cancer specialist. The doctor was very knowledgeable and caring, but to our horror, diagnosed her with lymphoma, the same cancer Bijou had.

The doctor was very concerned about Mom, and gently explained what lymphoma is. I already knew, but could not let on because Mom did not know Bijou had had lymphoma and despite undergoing treatments for months, did not have much time left. I did not want to upset her.

Mom's specialist told us about the standard chemotherapy treatment for lymphoma, but said he would not recommend giving that to someone Mom's age because of the unpleasant side effects and how ill she would feel.

"Oh, this cannot be happening," I thought.

We took Mom back to her primary-care doctor a couple of days later. He took her vital signs and immediately admitted her to the hospital because her blood pressure was very low. After some testing, they discovered one of her lymph glands was very swollen and bleeding and that was why her stools were black, they were full of darkened blood. She became very weak because of the loss of blood. The doctors gave her blood transfusions, then she stayed in the hospital about a week for testing.

It appeared the bleeding had stopped, so they recommended Mom go into a nursing home for some rehabilitation. Mom had been so active at home, so we thought perhaps the rehab exercises would help her, then we could take her home. Mom did not want to be in the hospital or nursing home, but agreed to go as long as she could go home afterwards.

While in the hospital, we met the chemo doctor, who explained generally about chemo. Then Mom was transferred to the nursing home.

Heartbreakingly, about that same time, Bijou died. He was one of the one percent for whom chemo did not work. I never could tell Mom about Bijou's illness or death from lymphoma, that would scare and upset her, but we did explain to her what her lymphoma was and what they wanted to do to her with chemo.

My brother was in favor of chemo at first, but listened to the concerns I had after doing my research. He borrowed some medical books and went to the Internet to do his own research. He then asked the cancer doctor if he would administer a lower dose of chemo chemicals to Mom because she was elderly and frail.

"No, I will give her full strength," he said.

My brother was appalled, and no longer in support of chemo for our elderly and frail Mom. We agreed it was Mom's decision as to whether she wanted chemo or not, and discussed with Mom what we had read, because we wanted her to be fully informed. Although she was elderly and frail, her mind was alert and clear. After listening to us, she had made up her mind.

"I am ninety-three now, and I have lived my life, a very good long life. I do not want to throw up, feel sick, and then lose my hair. Chemo may get me sicker and not any better. It may just kill me. I do not want chemo treatments."

We respected and were supportive of her decision.

The subsequent reception for my Mom and us was not friendly after Mom told the doctors she did not want chemo. They immediately called a family meeting with the nursing home administrator, social worker, nurses and related staff, Mom, William, and me.

The administrator was evidently displeased with her decision. He looked at me and sternly said, "I recommend you tell your Mother to get chemo," then immediately went on to say that he could file a medical complaint against me for giving my Mom vitamin C. I wondered if this somehow was a threat, but I knew I had done the right thing in trying to help my mother, and I would not be intimidated into making the wrong decision.

The team again recommended chemo, and when we reminded them of her decision, they said we should put Mom in hospice because she is in such bad shape and is losing her sense of reality. They claimed she did not know what was going on.

My brother and I were surprised at this claim, Mom was just fine earlier, so we insisted she was doing well. But they were right — Mom did seem disoriented right now and did not seem to be able to hear them. I asked to see her hearing aid to check it.

I immediately discovered they had replaced her hearing aid battery, but never took the plastic protective tab off the new battery, so the hearing aid was not working. No wonder Mom seemed disoriented! She was a 93-year-old woman surrounded by a dozen strangers who were talking *at* her, but she could not hear them.

I took the tab off the battery, Mom put the hearing aid in her ear, and she heard perfectly well. There was nothing wrong with Mom's mind. I felt so sorry for Mom, and glad we were there to help her. Then I felt sorry for all the elderly or ill people in similar situations who have no family or friends looking out for them.

CHAPTER 22

Another Storm

"The broken heart. You think you will die, but you just keep living, day after day after terrible day."

—*Charles Dickens, Great Expectations*

om hung in there, and William and I, and other family and friends, visited her every day at the nursing home. Relatives from near and far visited Mom and made her day, including her niece Pat from Nevada and her grandson Zachary from Pittsburgh. We watched her favorite television shows such as *Family Feud* and *Doctor Oz*, and of course, her beloved Yankee baseball games. How she loved Derek Jeter, A-Rod, Mariano Rivera and C.C. Sabathia. She knew the entire team, their batting averages, and latest successes. Together we saw Jeter get his 3,000th hit.

Mom would sometimes ask about Bijou, and I had to tell her he was doing fine. How could I tell her Bijou had contracted lymphoma, the same disease as her, and died within months of being diagnosed, despite going through the entire chemo protocol?

One day, Mom lost more blood from the bleeding tumor and had to go back to the hospital for another transfusion. The cancer specialist who originally diagnosed Mom with the lymphoma stopped by and told us emphatically that it would not be good to get chemo for our elderly Mom. He said the other doctors were making plans behind the scenes for Mom to get chemo, and they were not correct.

Mom was in the hospital for more than a week and was again stabilized. She knew what was to come, so wanted to go home to spend her last days being hospiced at home. Dad had always told Mom to stay in their house as long as she could, and she decided she wanted to go home and die there, not in a cold nursing home or hospital. She wanted to spend her last days in her own home, her own safe haven, her heaven on Earth.

So that's what we did. William promised to stay with her day and night, and I promised to go there every night after work to cook dinner for her, and on the weekend to give William some time to himself. William arranged for a hospital bed and regular nursing care, and off we went.

Mom was at home, in her castle, where she wanted to be. Her family, friends, and neighbors visited, and I took Rio to visit. He had visited her in the nursing home and did a marvelous job as a therapy dog in training. She loved to see him.

Later that month, Hurricane Irene hit New Jersey. Joe was in sunny Italy on a two-week business trip. He had been traveling a lot the last few years and was gone sometimes for weeks at a time, leaving me feeling alone more than I liked. I visited Mom the day before the storm hit and returned home that night to feed and take care of Rio and Shaman.

I heard the strong winds grow with ferocity through the night as I tried to get a few hours of sleep at home. Just what we did not need now was a hurricane. None of us could sleep with the noise of the strong winds and heavy rain. I just sat and hugged Rio and Shaman, getting a lot of comfort and giving them all I could. We finally fell asleep out of pure exhaustion.

Our electrical power went out at about three a.m. I awoke and something told me to check our basement. I found a flashlight and went to check it. It never used to flood, but in the last few years, from both the overdevelopment in our area and the more frequent and increasingly severe storms, water had started to enter the basement after heavy rainfalls.

We had invested in French drains and a sump pump and were so happy about that. We felt secure. But when I went down to the basement, I heard nothing. Of course not. We had no electricity and the pumps were not running.

I called Joe in Italy.

"We do have a battery backup, right? I can just put a new battery in?"

"No, we do not," he told me.

Exhausted and alone, and completely in the dark except for my little flashlight, I began to feel defeated.

Everything in the basement was now in a foot of water. I quickly unplugged all the electrical plugs to be safe, just in case. Then I bailed out dozens and dozens of buckets of water into the sink drain, but the water was coming in faster than I could bail it out.

I lifted as many treasured possessions as I could and put them in a higher place so they could dry. I had little choice but to give up on the rest. The storm was horrible and the only things that kept me sane were my dogs and my cell phone, the only lifeline I had with my Mom, William, and the rest of the world.

I texted William and told him how bad the storm was by us and that I would try to come by later when the worst part of the storm passed. My trip turned out to be quite an adventure.

What a nightmare it was, the entire 13-mile drive to Mom's house. Trees and electrical wires were down, and roads were closed everywhere. I had to detour from every road I would normally take because they were all closed, blocked by police cars or with trees and wires down, and then I had to detour from those detours. Emergency vehicles were everywhere, trying to direct traffic, but not knowing where they were sending people.

I finally made it to Mom's house. It took over one and one-half hours to travel what normally took 25 minutes.

Mom was out of power too, but William and I managed to keep her cool, comfortable and well fed. Finally, the power went back on a day or so later at Mom's house, and things went back to normal and stayed that way for weeks.

Then on the evening of September 26, 2011, as I went to leave for home after visiting Mom and making her dinner, I wished Mom a good night and kissed her. Though she was weak, she stared at me with her dreamy green eyes and whispered sweetly like she had done so many times before, but a bit more weakly now, "Joanie, be careful." Always a caring Mom. Once a mother, always a mother.

I drove home and got some sleep. It was almost six a.m. when I was awakened by the phone. It was William.

"Mom passed about five a.m.," he said. Though we knew this was coming soon, we both cried. It was about one month since Mom had come home from the hospital.

I drove to Mom's right away, my life with her and so many wonderful memories flashing before me. I cried. Mom was now gone from us too, now in her heaven with Dad and Pat and everyone else who left before, looking down on us and smiling.

William and I were devastated. Losing Mom marked the end of a wonderful era; we couldn't believe she was gone. How we missed her blessed presence, and forever will.

It suddenly occurred to me that the date was September 27. 9/27. How interesting, surely it is a date with significance … September is my brother's birthday month, and my sister Pat's favorite number — and her birth date — was 27. A coincidence?

"Not at all," I thought.

William had stayed with Mom during her illness until her last day, and I know Mom was forever grateful for that, as I am. It was wonderful of him to help her in her last months.

Mom's funeral was joyful, with her favorite music playing and many of her photos and paintings, as well as lots of chrysanthemum flowers, "mums," decorating the room. She took with her a big piece of our hearts. I hoped she would smile down on us now and then.

All of this was followed at the end of October, a few days before Halloween, by a freak snowstorm which came to be known as Snowtober. It dumped a lot of heavy, wet snow on branches of trees still covered with leaves. The snow added extra weight to the trees already laden with leaves, so branches and trees throughout our area broke in half and fell to the ground, taking down electrical wires, blocking roads, and causing mass power outages. We were out of power for about 10 days again, still without a generator.

William was tending to things at Mom's house and came up to stay with us for a while.

Interestingly, some of the news stations called the storm "Storm Alfred." Alfred was my Dad's name, my Mom's beloved husband. Another coincidence? Perhaps.

CHAPTER 23

Chaos of Growing Up

*"Chaos sometimes awakens sleeping parts of us and
leads to amazing changes."*

—Joni

William returned to Pittsburgh, and Joe was still travelling internationally. With Mom gone, I felt so lonesome. My heart was shattered. I plunged to a very low place, depressed and saddened by so much loss in such a short time — Pat, Aunt Jane, Marly, Bijou, and now Mom, all in a year and a half. They had been such a big part of my life, and I spent so much of my time with them, such beautiful souls. I felt incredibly alone and empty without them. I had lost a huge part of myself, my heart, and my world with their passings, and I felt so isolated. The loss of them affected me more than I had ever imagined possible.

My world was suddenly out of balance, in a state of chaos, nothing was settled. I never had time to mourn any of them. There had been no time for closure. My typically well-balanced Libra self was now totally out-of-balance. My life seemed to have lost much of its meaning. I felt my purpose in life, my focus, dreams, and desires had vanished. Nothing seemed to matter anymore. It felt like some unknown power was sucking all the life out of me. Unknown to me at the time, this was to become a massive life-changing experience.

Mom and Pat had been my two best buddies, my pals, confidants, always there for me and each other no matter how rough times were, always my number one cheerleaders and supporters in anything I tried to do. We confided in each other, and though we had our ups and downs, we loved each other so much.

There is something very special about a mother's love and the bond between close sisters. Mom's heart especially was always full of love, joy, and never-ending support. She was so full of common sense and wisdom, the strong matriarch of our family. As President Lincoln wrote, "All that I am, and hope to be, I owe to my angel Mother." And I believe in that.

My sister was always happy and smiling, until she got very sick, and even then she would greet us with big smiles when she could. She loved us all, and only wished good things for us. We were never rich financially, but together, we were rich in every other way. How I missed Pat and Mom!

Joe and William helped me through my grief, but they were dealing with their own sadness at the loss of Pat and Mom, their demanding jobs, commitments, and personal problems. Everyone has their own baggage, and I certainly was feeling mine. I became very confused and was not very good at communicating with anyone, not even myself. Sometimes I felt I was on the verge of losing my mind.

Space separated all of us as well. Joe continued traveling internationally for work for weeks at a time and frequently was not home. He was in Japan for three weeks, then China, Europe, South and Central America, Pakistan, India, and the list went on. William was in Pittsburgh, so we kept in touch by phone, but it wasn't the same as being together in person.

Besides, as the book by John Gray suggests, *Men Are From Mars, Women Are From Venus*, aren't they? I don't think they realized how deeply I was affected by the loss of Pat and Mom and that I was sinking to a new low. And even if they did, I do not know if they would have known how to help me. I certainly did not. Other family and good friends tried to help too. Bottom line, if I needed to talk to someone, someone was always there. If I needed anything, one of them was there.

Everyone helping me were angels in their own special ways, and it helped a lot speaking with them and sharing. Like everyone else, I needed to feel cared about and desired a lot of old-fashioned, tender loving care, and good communication and respect. They gave that to me, but when they left to take care of their own lives and families, I crept back to my sadness. They did what they could, but nothing was lifting me out of my sorrow.

Some people tried to help by telling me to turn to God. My belief in my supreme being, my God, was still there and at times I turned to there, most often when I was alone and time seemed to stand still. But something was still missing. I was still in a very low place.

Does time heal everything? Maybe, but it does not always happen, and it does not always happen fast. Whoever said it does, I think, was a bit out of touch. The days and nights passed by, but time did not ease the pain.

I came to the sharp realization that sometimes we get so caught up in our daily lives, with multiple jobs, school, and other commitments we make, that we lose sight of those who are dearest to us, who may need our help most. One day, we open our eyes, only to find it is too late because for one reason or another, they are gone.

I opened my eyes and felt guilty for not being there more for my Mom and Pat when they needed me. I was always so busy with school, with work, and my own home duties. I berated myself for not being more helpful to them. I gave myself a nice guilt trip.

∞

I plodded through each day the best I could. Despite being busy at work, with housework, and home life, and with some dog training and shows here and there, when the days faded quietly into night, and at other times when I had too much time to think, I found myself very sad still. I was still broken-hearted, and did not want to go on.

I thought of how tumultuous life had been, and felt I understood now what people meant after someone died and they said, "They are now at rest." Pat and Mom were resting after their terrible bouts with cancer.

I felt horrible and wanted to rest too, to shut out everything. I was so sad and it was so hard to get out of bed in the morning. I would open my eyes, then dread what the day would bring. I wondered what was next, and didn't feel the energy to go on. But I had to go on. Taking my own life was not an option. I was not there yet. It was not my time.

For fleeting moments, I wondered if what I was going through was depression. This may have been depression, but I did not for a moment consider seeing a doctor or therapist. I saw no use in seeing a doctor, from family and friends' experiences. I believed a doctor visit would only result in a drug prescription and would not address the cause of my problem.

What I was feeling was not something drugs would heal. I needed — and wanted — to heal from within, not mask whatever it was. I did not want to take drugs and get hooked on them, or experience side effects that seem to happen to so many people, especially from freely prescribed opioid drugs.

I thought there might be some kind of alternative medicine that might assist me. I knew meditation and yoga would be very beneficial in so many ways, both mentally and physically. Oh, and a massage would make me feel good and take some anxiety away. There are so many other types of activities you can do to help yourself. Perhaps some kind of alternative medicine would indeed help along the way, but I felt I needed to get at the root cause of my issues.

After many hours, days and weeks of deep thinking, I finally came to the realization that I was going through a major change in my life. That is why I felt like I did. It made more sense now.

One of the doctors who treated Mom told William that we never really grow up until our mothers pass away. Perhaps a good part of what I was feeling were the growing pains from finally being thrown out of the nest, so to speak, and having to really grow up and transition from my life with Mom and Pat. I believed it was time for me to get out and create my new life without them, do things in my own way, and finally evolve to become what and who I was meant to be.

Yes, it was time to do so, I quickly discovered.

This revelation became a key turning point in my life and a major life-changing experience. I realized that to find my new life of fulfillment, I needed to create my own independent life. I needed to find out who I was meant to be. Not Mom's daughter or Pat's sister, but Joan.

What a scary idea! I was clearly now on my own and had to develop into the person I was meant to be. I had to keep growing.

I needed to get out into the world and look for self-fulfillment and new opportunities, because they were not going to find me. I needed to discover what I was meant to be doing. I did a lot of reading and understood that to attain anything good, I needed to focus on good positive thoughts, and with that, good positive energy would come. Sitting around was not the cure for whatever I had. It was not an option.

Though I did not know where to start, I decided I would get out, try new things, and keep busy, even if the new activities merely distracted me from my sadness for a while. Distractions, as Pat said, can be very helpful to get through sadness.

"Where will all of this take me?" I wondered. I didn't know, but life dared me to trust it and take a giant leap, so I did.

CHAPTER 24

Let's Go Mum!

"Sometimes a very special soul enters your life and quickly turns it upside down, very much for the better."

—Joni

Rio and Shaman stepped up and helped me through this difficult time. They were always by my side. Shaman, now in his last days, was a dear and loving pup right to the end.

Rio selflessly tried to make up for everything. He was always grinning and elf-like, delivering unconditional love and much-needed kisses and jumping up in pure joy just at the sight of me. He helped me keep much of my sanity during this phase of my life.

It was about this time, after the passing of Mom and my recognizing the need for change in my life, that I noticed Rio had been nudging my arm with his nose a lot more than usual lately, and putting his front paws on me more and more. He was much more persistent in getting my attention, and he wanted to be with me all the time.

Rio also wanted to get out and do things, not sit home like a couch potato. He obviously liked the show activity and wanted to go somewhere every day to have fun.

In retrospect, he was taking responsibility for me and emphatically telling me, "Time to move on Mum, we are here and now, so let's enjoy life! And dear Mum, please do not be so sad."

Rio nudged me again and looked at me intently, asking, "Can we do something now Mum? Let's go, there is so much to do, and not enough time to do it all. Let's hurry."

I laughed.

"Yes, Rio, let's go out and do some training outside. Yes, let's go do things together, my dear boy."

Then I suddenly had a small — or maybe not so small — revelation. Yes, I decided that while I was trying new activities and creating my new self, perhaps getting out, training, competing at shows and trials and meeting new people would help me. Maybe it would keep me busy, distract me, and maybe, just maybe, some new goals and dreams would come out of this and I would find a new meaning to life.

I did not know if that was the answer, but I knew I needed to do something to keep busy and keep my sanity. Sitting home moping definitely was not the answer.

It turns out, in my search to keep busy, I found my own form of alternative medicine to help me on my path forward and get me through this very difficult time. That alternative medicine came in the form of a very special spirit — Rio, who added a much-needed spark to my life and brought me new opportunities galore!

Surprisingly, Rio knew more about what I should do and what was best for me than I. Unlike most humans, dogs do not dwell so much on the past or worry about the future. They live in the current moment. I think a lot of us can learn from our dogs. And as I was to find out quickly, Rio was right about me getting out, keeping busy, and making new friends.

Rio was surely on to something, or should I say, up to something! He tried, and was usually successful, in getting more and more of my attention each day. He seemed driven now, as if he had some special plans for me. He surprised me the first time he went up to the kitchen door that leads to our garage and stood still, nose pointing to the door, asking me to take him somewhere.

"Please Mum, let's go out today, okay? Can we go for a ride to a show? Or can we go to training, Mum? Can we go now, Mum?"

It was clear Rio wanted to be with me, and he wanted me to go places with him. Every day. So, I obliged, and off we went to more and more training classes, shows, and trials.

He began staring at me more frequently, as if to communicate with me, sometimes poking me with his front paw to try to tell me something I did not quite understand, but was so very willing to learn.

What amazed me was that I really did start to understand Rio more and more each day. This entire process became very interesting, as I had never become so close to a dog — or any animal — before.

Rio began to take on a big personality. Or perhaps I should say, I had just awakened and took notice of a special soul with a large, very special personality. I recalled Kate had joked with me once that she noticed that I, like her, view Tervuren as people. Now I more fully understood what she meant. Rio, like other Tervs, has an extraordinary spirit, humor, playfulness, and intelligence about him, and a devotion to his favorite people. Some say Tervs are elf-like, others consider them people-like in many ways.

Although I am a person and Rio is a dog, we both seemed to have discovered a new-found respect for each other and began to communicate at a new, much higher level. As such, I began to look at my angel Rio in a different light. We started to hang out together more and became more involved in dog sports. We became very close. As we spent more and more time together, Rio and I became even closer and accepted each other as we are. In fact, we became inseparable.

There then came a point when I realized that Rio claimed me as all his. He began following me everywhere around the house, watching my every move, and listening to each word I spoke as if he understood each one. Joe began calling Rio my shadow, and both of us twins, not always with approval, but rather with a bit of jealousy. I thought Rio and I were becoming more like soul mates. I did not realize it at the time, but Rio had become my strength, someone I could rely on who was always there for me. And Rio knew it.

As time went on, it was clear Rio had decided I was the one for him, and he wanted to own me. He wanted all of my time, attention and love, often to Joe's dismay. Rio took to me so much that Joe thought Rio was becoming obsessed with me and very possessive. "Very possessive" — that description was in the American Kennel Club Belgian Tervuren breed standard, too.

This was all quite uplifting for me. I was getting my daily tender loving care, and I felt more joy, more completeness. I now had a lot of goals, having committed to helping Rio get his conformation Championship. I had zest for life again. I thought, as someone very wise had said, "In my darkest hour I reached out for a hand and I found a paw."

I continued to sign up for more shows with Rio, despite the fact we were still not winning. I thought of Mom and how she knew how much showing Rio meant to me. She had been very sad that we were not winning in the conformation ring. One of the last things Mom advised me to do before she passed away was to, "Give up with the dog-show thing."

Perhaps Mom was right. Maybe we should stop.

"But Mom," I thought, "we just cannot stop now." I believed the odds were in our favor that Rio would start winning soon!

CHAPTER 25

The Champp

"Don't ever give up on your dreams — believe, focus,
and try hard, and your dreams will become reality."

—Joni

Spending time with Rio, training and showing Rio, became my main focus and distraction. Rio inspired me so much every day, and quite simply, made me very happy. I felt absolutely needed and unconditionally loved. I really loved this.

When I awoke, Rio was always by my side, staring into my eyes with his sweet brown eyes.

"Let's get going Mum! We have got a lot to do today. Life is short! No time to waste! Let's go to the show!" he'd say.

So we did.

We both enjoyed getting out and going places, and most of all, spending lots of time together and meeting new friends. We traveled near and far in search of conformation shows with hopes of earning his American Kennel Club Championship someday soon. Erwinna,

Gilbert, Macungie, Ludwig's Corner, and Wrightstown, Pennsylvania. West Windsor, Morristown, Ringoes, Augusta, Bridgewater, and Freehold, New Jersey. Staten Island, Stormville, and Oyster Bay, New York. It was exciting to go to so many places I had never been before, especially with my buddy Rio.

Then, as if it were a gift from Mom, just weeks after her passing, Rio won his first three points and his first major win in the conformation ring.

Kate and Jeff, Rio's breeders, had called to say they were coming down from Connecticut to show one of their new dogs in the Augusta show. I had entered Rio in that very show and was now more nervous than ever. My stomach sank. Maybe I shouldn't go to this show? I was trying so hard, but maybe I was just not doing a good enough job with their boy? We still were not winning any points, not to mention winning any majors, and it surely was my fault, as Rio is a gorgeous dog, of exceptional breeding. Surely it was my handling? Of course, that was it. I was not graceful enough, and not doing Rio justice.

Kate and Jeff arrived with their gorgeous show dogs. I was very nervous, sure we would once again not win any points. After exchanging greetings, I set the stage for our sure upcoming loss by telling them over and over that, "We are getting better… we should get points soon … we should get a major soon. It will happen, but do not expect it today. Rio's coat needs to fill out more. We will do the best we can today, but please do not expect anything."

We had shown the day before against another class dog and lost. Today, we had four dogs in the ring, including the dog we had lost to yesterday. On top of it, one of the dogs was Kate and Jeff's magnificent dog. We were surely doomed.

The steward called us into the ring. My heart raced, and I filled with emotion. "Come Rio, let's give this one our best try for Pat and Mom!"

I proudly entered the ring with my buddy Rio by my side. I tried to keep him engaged by chattering happily and being more animated than usual. He kept his eyes on me more than usual, wondering, "What is she up to today?" He could sense my excitement.

"All around!" the judge called out. We all ran around the ring, then lined up in order. Then we went around the ring one at a time and stacked, then did our out-and-back and stacked again.

I did my best. I ran as well as I could, trying to show off Rio's lovely gait. We did a good out-and-back and Rio stacked very nicely for the judge.

When we lined up for the final view by the judge, I stacked Rio, then stood beside him, smiling proudly, holding his show lead high up in the air as if to say, "Pick my boy, please! Please pick my boy Rio!"

Rio looked at me, wide-eyed in wonder. The judge looked up and down the line at all the handsome Terv boys.

Suspense … it seemed like minutes before the judge finally made her selection. Then, to my surprise, I heard the judge call out, "Winners Dog!" She was pointing to Rio! A loud cheer from friends and friendly competitors resonated through the ring.

Wow! A three-point major win! Rio's first points ever, and his first major! We did it! I was so happy for him … for us … I was stunned!

Rio could sense my excitement and was joyful.

"I have no idea what is going on, but I am so happy that you are happy Mum! I love you, Mum!" he said.

Kate and Jeff were thrilled, friends hugged me, and fellow competitors shook my hand. I was sad Joe was not there to see this. He went to some of the shows, but generally was not interested in accompanying us.

Rio and I went home, and we all celebrated. I was ecstatic for weeks! I wondered if this was a gift from Mom and Pat?

Weeks later, Rio went Best of Winners at another show, another three-point major. We ended the year with a third major and a two-point minor, totaling eleven points. I was thrilled. We had the two majors we needed and just needed four more points to finish his American Kennel Club Championship.

We continued to enter dozens of shows and traveled throughout New Jersey, New York, and Pennsylvania to just about every show offered within three hours of home. Many times, Rio was the only dog entered, so no points were available. Often, Rio's only competition was one of the top two Tervuren dogs in the United States being handled by a well-known professional handler.

Rio was so close to finishing his Championship, and I was determined. Our points in the conformation ring did not come easy, but we were very entertaining, and we had a lot of people cheering for us. Rio was always a friendly representative of the Tervuren breed, wagging his tail and flirting with other dogs. He was just so happy to be there with the other canines. At times, he was quite a character. One time, Rio excitedly trotted around the ring, head to the ground like a lawnmower, probably smelling a bitch in heat and other fascinating scents, quite to the surprise and curiosity of the judge.

He was in doggie heaven, apologizing to me later, "Sorry Mum, there have been some lovely smelling gals and dogs here. I know you don't mind me smelling the show grounds just this once, huh, Mum?"

Other times, friendly Rio leaned on the judge, tail wagging, begging for a point or two to make me happy.

"Please Judge, would you give me a point for my Mum? She really would love me to get a point. I haven't gotten too many." Rio certainly has a lot of personality.

Also entertaining was when my macho Rio teenager became mesmerized by a Belgian lass, and with tail wagging, eyes sparkling, and wearing a charming grin, he tried to fascinate her with his paw tapping dance. Mystified by the bitch's standoffishness and teasing, he flopped to the ground enchanted and quite exhausted.

I was often thrilled to receive compliments from spectators, competitors and judges alike.

"What a handsome man!"

"How good-natured!"

"Great movement!"

"Wonderful personality."

Many show spectators wished for a dog like him, and oh, so many observers told us, "We picked him — he should have won." I too believed in my Rio. In hopes of Rio's final Championship points, I entered the Bridgewater show weekend. Rio now had three majors and just needed four points. On the first day of the show, Rio earned a point over the other class dog.

On the next day, Rio earned one point over the class dog. Now he only needed two points to finish his Championship. I was hopeful he would earn another point over the class dog on the last day of the show. The judge was from Finland. I prayed this European judge would like Rio's European look and award Rio Winners Dog over the other class dog. That would give us one of the two points he still needed for his Championship.

We arrived early and waited outside the ring, but I did not see the other class dog. We waited anxiously, and it was now almost time to go into the ring.

I still did not see the other class dog. There were six Tervs entered, but so far only two other dogs, a Champion and a Grand Champion, showed up. Oh well, we were here. We would show anyway, even if there were no other class dogs.

I decided to just let Rio have fun and be happy. He was in a good mood as always, and wanted to flirt with the other dogs, so I let him enjoy himself. He had fun smiling at some of the bitches in other breeds, wagging his tail in glee.

We waited patiently. The judge was judging another breed inside the ring. Was I mistaken, or did she take a look or two at Rio outside the ring, flirting with another dog, tail wagging in his happy way?

The judge finished judging that breed, then it was time for the Tervuren. The ring steward called the class dogs into the ring. Turned out, we were it. The other class dog did not show up.

The judge started out by apologizing that Rio and I did not have any competition. I smiled and said, "That's okay."

"Oh well, no points for us today. I will just let Rio have some fun," I thought.

I took Rio around the ring, and he did his stack and the out-and-back, then again around the ring. The judge did her inspection of him, awarded him Best Open Dog and Best of Winners, then instructed us to stand in the corner behind the Champions, also known as "specials," who were lined up for judging.

She wanted us to wait for the Best of Breed judging for which we had qualified. She began to judge the specials.

I decided to make the best of our time in the ring by letting Rio just have a good time. He caught sight of a pretty Belgian Sheepdog waiting at the gate for her turn in the ring. His ears went up, focusing on her, and he started flirting with her from a distance, standing excitedly in a perfect stack, focused on her, tail wagging.

Rio grinned and said sweetly, "Hello, young lady, you are very pretty today. I would love to meet you. Aren't I handsome?" Rio was in heaven wagging his tail at her. He puffed up his chest, head up, mouth smiling, and his tail wagged so hard I thought he might fall over.

I laughed. Rio seems to find girlfriends wherever he goes. He is so charming and gentle with the gals, and they usually love him, even those gals that typically don't give male dogs the time of day.

Meanwhile, the judge asked one special, then the other, to go around the ring. I started to watch more closely. Was it my imagination — was she looking at Rio, then back at the specials where they were lined up? I must have been imagining that.

The judge finished up with the specials then called Rio into line after them. Then she approached me and said something I just could not hear.

"Pardon me?" I asked.

"BEST OF BREED — please stand over there," the judge instructed me.

Oh my God! Oh my dog! Rio won Best of Breed over two specials! Two points! Rio finished his Championship!

The judge shook my hand and told me that Rio has an exceptional temperament. In my joy, and to both her and my surprise, I then proceeded to give her a hug! Then lots of hugs to Rio.

I was so overjoyed that Rio finally did it. Rio finished his Championship in about a year and a half. He was now an American Kennel Club Champion!

I wish Joe and William had seen this, but Joe could not make it and my brother was back home in Pittsburgh. My Mom and my sister Pat would have loudly cheered us on if they were here, and perhaps they were.

Someone later told me that when someone passes, they continue to send us love and gifts when we need them most. I thought of Mom and Pat. Yes, they probably were behind Rio's Championship, knowing how much this would mean to me. I would bet they were indeed watching over us, sending love and magic, helping us to finally do this!

I looked back over the last year and a half. Rio and I had competed at many shows and made many good friends in many different breeds, including the Belgians. Rio's breeders, my friend Cathy who shows Boston

Terriers, kind instructors, owner-handlers, and professional handlers had eagerly stepped up to offer advice, from diet to show-ring tips.

Things unknown to us became familiar with constant training, daily practice, and watching the pros. I am so grateful to all of you in the dog show community who helped us achieve Rio's Championship in the conformation ring; I cannot thank you enough. You have helped me move on with my life and opened up new doors and opportunities for us, including writing this book, something I would never have imagined. I send you my heartfelt thanks.

I encourage anyone who considers showing your show dog to do it. Just get out there, take some lessons, and do it! It is a magnificent sport and an honor to be in the show ring with your dog. I was nervous to compete the first time, and always got butterflies in my stomach. But I loved being out there with my best friend Rio, and all our efforts as a team resulted in building a closer relationship between us.

Rio and I showed in limited shows in the Best of Breed competition before we moved on to compete exclusively in dog performance sports. Before we did, I committed to showing Rio at least one time at the Westminster Dog Show in New York City, because he is a marvelous dog and through our trials and tribulations, that darling boy earned it. Rio was now a Champion, and he deserved to run in that ring with the other beautiful Tervuren. I never wanted to look back and regret not having showed at Westminster with him.

Boy oh boy, we are here now and only have so many years together, so let's go Rio! Rio agreed with me. We promised each other we would show at Westminster one day.

CHAPTER 26

Good Citizen Meets Romeo

"Sometimes you lose one angel and are blessed to meet another - I welcome you into my family and will always take care of you."

—*Joni*

Just after Rio earned his American Kennel Club Championship, I saw an advertisement on the Internet for an American Kennel Club Canine Good Citizen Test (CGC). It was scheduled to be held at a local pet store in our area. I signed Rio up immediately and researched the requirements for the test.

A ten-step test, it is not competitive; rather, your dog, if he passes all ten parts of the test, earns the American Kennel Club CGC title. The training for this test, which is obedience-based, is a good stepping stone for entry into sports like rally and obedience.

The ten parts of the CGC test at the time included: inspection by the evaluator of the dog's grooming and cleanliness, accepting a friendly stranger, sitting for petting by a stranger, walking on a loose lead with the handler, walking through a crowd of people, doing a sit and stay on command, coming when called, showing polite behavior around other dogs, supervised separation from the handler, and a demonstration of reaction to distractions.

Rio and I took the test as a team. I was nervous, but Rio did a very nice job. He was friendly with the evaluator and dogs involved in the test and was very well-behaved and did everything the evaluator asked. He earned the title of CGC!

We received a lovely CGC ribbon from the evaluator, plus an impressive American Kennel Club CGC certificate in the mail. I was also able to order a CGC rosette, pin, and badge from the American Kennel Club website for Rio's scrapbook and memory wall I had started.

Rio then passed the American Kennel Club Community Canine test (CGCA), which is the advanced level of the CGC test. The goal of the test is to evaluate the dog's skills in a natural setting like a show, training class, or community.

Then, at the Belgian Tervuren National in Gettysburg, Pennsylvania, Rio passed the American Kennel Club Urban Canine Good Citizen test (CGCU). Some consider this test a variation of the Canine Good Citizen test, performed in an urban setting. What a good boy you are, Rio!

It was about this time that Shaman took a quick turn for the worse. It was very sudden. One day, he just did not want to eat. We took him to the vet, and they did a variety of tests all day, but did not find anything wrong with him. They asked if we could leave him overnight for observation, so we did.

Sadly, he passed away early the next morning, before we arrived. We all believed it was cancer again. Shaman was such a sweet dog, and we loved him so. We were so glad that we rescued him and were honored to have him as our buddy. We were glad to have shared a life full of fun with him for many years.

We were heartbroken to lose him, but heeding Pat's instructions, weeks later we did a search on Petfinder and other sites on the Internet for another long-haired black German Shepherd. A new dog would never replace Shaman, as my sister had told me, but a new dog in our home would somehow distract us from much of the pain of losing him.

We searched for several days and located breeders, but we preferred to rescue a dog and save a life. We finally located a one-year-old long-haired black German Shepherd named Foxon in Virginia, at the All-American Mutt Rescue.

We contacted them and were asked to complete an application, which we promptly did. We provided references as requested, including friends, co-workers, and our veterinarian, so were shocked when we received a prompt denial.

In tears, I called the rescue to ask why, and was told it was because our application advised that we had an unneutered dog in our house — Rio. It showed that we were irresponsible. I told them Rio is a show dog and cannot be neutered. They accepted my answer, as it made sense to them, and proceeded to contact our references, all of whom were very positive. Our veterinarian even told them that Foxon had, "Just hit the lottery," in that he had found a very good family who wanted to adopt him and would take great care of him for the rest of his life. Cindy from the rescue contacted to advise that we could rescue Foxon. We were thrilled!

We made arrangements to meet a dog-rescue shuttle who would drive Foxon up from Virginia and meet us about a half hour from our house. We drove up Route 78 to meet him at a rest stop. We greeted the driver and thanked her profusely; without her it would have been a very long ride down to Virginia. She thanked us for rescuing Foxon and promptly brought him out of a crate from inside the van.

Out came the most gorgeous, black, long-haired Shepherd I had ever seen, and the most frightened and confused dog I had ever met. Foxon did not know what to make of anything, having been put up for rescue six months before, and now he was being relocated again. We tried to calm Foxon and offered him treats, but he was too nervous to eat anything. We gently coaxed Foxon into our car for the ride home. None of us knew what we were in for.

Foxon was very shy, frightened, and confused, and rightfully so. The American Kennel Club papers that accompanied him said he was one-year-old, born in an American Kennel Club German Shepherd litter. Unfortunately, a breeder of show dogs would have little use for a German Shepherd dog who was born black with a very long coat. Simply, Foxon did not meet the breed standard.

Foxon was given up to the rescue at six months old, largely unsocialized. The rescue took very good care of him for another six months and did an excellent job in promptly placing him, as they do with many other dogs in need. We were lucky to rescue him. Time is proving that his breeder's loss was a gigantic gain for Foxon and us.

First, we had to address Foxon's fears. It was immediately apparent that Foxon was not socialized when he was very young, during a very critical period of a dog's life. He was very afraid of us and would not make good eye contact with us for months.

I signed him up for different training classes with the goal of socializing, training, and giving him all the love and support he needed to build confidence and be happy. Before we started the classes, we wanted to change his name. The first names Joe came up with were Radar and

Snowshoe. He chose those names because Foxon was so underweight that his ears and paws looked significantly oversized. I thought Radar and Snowshoe were very funny names, but did not want to call him either name.

I wanted a special name for this scared boy, an exceptional name that when people heard it, they would smile and send him positive energy and happy emotions. Maybe that would help diminish his fears.

We decided to call him Romeo. It turned out to be a perfect name, because when people hear it they usually smile and feel love for this darling rescue. They often want to say, "Hello, dear Romeo," to him and pet him, quickly creating a positive environment for him where he easily feels accepted by strangers.

CHAPTER 27

Rally On!

*"Sometimes it is the trials and tribulations of life
that define your character."*

—*Joni*

I discovered rally obedience while waiting to go into the show ring at one of the conformation shows. I found the trials intriguing. Teams of people and their dogs walked one at a time around the ring, looking very thoughtfully at signs and doing sits, jumps, circles, and some curious things that piqued my interest. I watched the dogs in the ring performing for quite some time and was in awe of their precise performances and attention to their handlers.

My show friends told me that performance sports like rally, obedience, and agility trials were often held at the same time as some of the conformation shows. A lot of people enjoy participating in performance sports because you can have fun with your dog and earn titles, even if your dog does not come in first in its competitive class, unlike conformation. All you need to do is qualify enough times (each qualifying score is known as a "leg"), in whatever sport your dog is doing, and your dog will get a title. If your dog scores high enough to be one of the top dogs in the trial, he or she may earn placement ribbons and other awards.

I was encouraged to try rally because my research on the Internet suggested it was a very rewarding dog sport, and can be one of the easier performance sports when you are first starting out with training and competition. I decided Rio and I would give it a try.

Some of the available venues include the American Kennel Club, United Kennel Club, and World Cynosport Rally, as well as some cyber groups on the Internet that offer titles via video. I also learned that rally obedience classes were offered nearby at St. Hubert's Dog Training School, and signed Rio up for their next available class.

Carole, our instructor, was very knowledgeable and patient with all her students, and provided an excellent positive training environment. She gave all of us copies of the signs for both the American Kennel Club and World Cynosport Rally, which I studied carefully.

In class, Rio did well with the rally obedience signs we needed to perform, but I quickly discovered he was not always very motivated or driven. At times, I found it very hard to keep Rio's attention when running a course, especially when his fellow student, a darling Belgian Shepherd bitch, was present. I did not have Rio from a pup, so I missed the early food and toy training that many people are lucky to do with their young dogs that results in consistent high motivation and focus in the trial ring. Thus Rio is not consistently food-driven, and as I discovered, he is not toy-driven at all.

When I told this to my instructors, I knew they thought I was making it up. More than one has told me, "Of course Rio is food-driven! You just do not have the right foods!"

I used all kinds of dog treats, from juicy fresh-cooked steak, organic hot dogs, liver, meatballs, to cheese, and the most popular doggie junk foods, treats other dogs would drool for, all with random success. If something worked well for a few minutes one day in training class, it did not work the next time I tried it.

Although food was not a consistent motivator for Rio in training classes, it was usually helpful at home while training, when he was less distracted by other dogs and new scents. So I used food as a motivator when Rio was in the mood for it at home or class, and when he was not interested in food, I had to try something else.

In lieu of food, I tried using toys, but Rio is even less excited about toys than he is about food. When we got him, I tried to play ball and Frisbee with him, but he ran away from me, giving me an odd look as if to say, "Why are you throwing those things at me? What have I done to deserve this?"

Despite explaining all of this to our many instructors, some of them refused to give up. Our awesome instructor Niki went out and bought a bag full of interactive toys she was sure would fix this problem. We gave it our best try, but Rio promptly looked at me and said, "Thank you very much, Mum, but I am just not interested in these things."

Despite this, I would not give up. I began to improvise and use alternative positive rewards. After much effort, I discovered that the best alternative reward proved to be me, my love and animation.

We trained with Carole at St. Hubert's for many months, and had a lot of fun learning and executing the rally signs for both the American Kennel Club and World

Cynosport Rally. Some are simple for many dogs, such as: Sit, Sit and Down, Sit and Stand, Sit and Walk Around, Left and Right Turns, 360 degree turns, and Slow/Fast/ Normal Pace. There are also more advanced signs which are often more complicated.

We practiced and practiced, then, as with conformation, there quickly came a time when I thought, "Let's give rally a go in competition," and entered Rio into an American Kennel Club trial in Ramsey.

There were many entries of both obedience and rally obedience dogs at the trial, and it was very crowded, thus quite noisy and intimidating for our first trial entry. People and dogs were everywhere, with many dogs left in crates so competitors could do their walkthroughs of the courses before they ran the course with their dogs. Some of the best competitors in the Tristate area were here with their well-trained dogs they had spent years training.

This was our first rally trial, actually our first trial of any kind, and I was very nervous though I knew we were well prepared for this. Little did I know these ring nerves would never go away for me! It became part of the excitement and fun of trialing and keeping us at our highest performance level. It was quickly our turn in the ring.

Rio and I went through the rally course. He heeled nicely next to me on lead and seemed to do really well, except for one hesitation with a sit. I did not think we missed any signs.

At the end of the course, the judge smiled and said, "Nice job, you have qualified!" I was elated!

Everyone finished their runs, then the judge called the qualifiers back in the ring. Rio earned a score of 95 out of 100 points! I was so proud of him. What a nice job for our first rally trial! Rio knew I was happy and gave me his sweet Rio smile as he wagged his tail.

We continued with rally, and over the course of a couple of years, Rio earned his American Kennel Club Rally Novice, Intermediate, Advanced, and Rally Advanced Excellent titles, which, at the time, were the only and highest of titles he could earn in American Kennel Club rally. What an honor it was to have achieved these titles with my darling boy Rio!

During our rally journey, we had our great and not-so-great moments, as with anything else. A few times, I was a complete klutz, walking right by and missing a sign that was right in front of my face, which resulted in a non-qualifying score or "NQ."

Perhaps the toughest NQ for me was the time I drove three hours with Rio in a snow storm into upstate New York for an American Kennel Club show. The storm had started halfway through our journey, and I decided to continue on to the show. On arrival I was grateful to be there, but a bit shaken up because the roads had been treacherous. I later discovered many cars and trucks had slid off the slippery road.

It was our turn. My heart was beating fast. I took a deep breath, then we entered the ring and started the course. Rio was on that day! We finished the course, and it felt good.

Then the judge came up to me. She told me we had a beautiful run, but unfortunately, I had missed one sign. I walked right by it, so we did not qualify. Rio was perfect, and I was the letdown that day.

Rio had his moments too, like the time we trialed on an outdoor course. It was a lovely course, but there were apparently some really interesting scents on the grass — maybe goose poop or animals walked through that area the night before. Or better yet for him, maybe there was a bitch in heat walking the course at some point.

Rio did every sign on the course for me, but in between each sign, his head went down and he sniffed the course very closely. Though he completed the course, he did not look at me consistently, so the judge NQ'd us for not working as a team. Rio apologized; he just could not control himself. From that experience, I learned quickly not to enter outdoor trials.

I learned our strengths and weaknesses and tried to work around them. I learned to laugh at myself and Rio after tough moments, love him all the more, and move on to the next trial.

We moved from American Kennel Club rally to the World Cynosport Rally venue. It is similar to American Kennel Club rally as far as many of the signs go, but there are different rules, bonus signs and extra points available in World Cynosport Rally, and a bonus for us, as all of our local venues are inside. We found the participants and judges to be very nice, making it a joy to participate.

Rio quickly earned a number of titles in World Cynosport Rally, including his Rally Level 1 and 2, with Awards of Excellence for earning all of his scores over 190 (out of a possible 210 points). He later earned his Rally Level 1 and 2 Championships.

To my surprise, Rio ranked third in the world in the World Cynosport Rally Year End Rankings in 2013 for his Level 1 Championship (RL1X)! I am so proud of him. And as icing on the cake, Kellar's Canine Academy, one of the trial clubs we show at, honored the dogs that regularly trial at their venue that had earned 2013 year-end top rankings. Kellar's had commemorative plaques made up to honor these dogs and awarded the plaques to the dogs and their owners at their annual Tournament trials the following year.

Next, we entered the United Kennel Club rally venue. It proved to be a very pleasant venue with very nice people as well, and we enjoyed it immensely. Rio earned his Rally Obedience 1 level title, earning the United Kennel Club title UR01.

We then took a break from the rally ring for a while to focus on other sports. The main reason was that Rio told me, "Mum, I am getting bored with all these repetitive sits and downs. Can we do something more exciting?" So, we took a break and signed up for training classes for sports like nose work, tracking, sheep herding, and doggie dancing!

*Rio enjoying the beach at Sandy Hook Gateway National
Recreation Area, specks of sand on his face*

Rio at a training class at Kellar's Canine Academy

Rio earns his American Kennel Club Championship!

Rio makes friends with a few horses at Lisa's training school farm and blows one of his new friends a kiss

Rio makes friends with a resident camel while taking a break from sheep herding

*Rio making friends with the fish in the hospice reception area —
they are so curious about each other!*

Rio enjoying an evening at Bark in the Park at a Somerset Patriot's baseball game

Rio and Romeo enjoying a ride in the car on the way to training class

Rio enjoyed playing in the yard during a snow storm. This photo earned "BEST in SNOW" in an on-line photo contest.

Rio knows he made Mum very proud, having earned his World Cynosport Rally ARCHX title

Rio posing after visiting and cheering up residents at the hospice

Rio enjoying the moment at the Belgian Tervuren National in Gettysburg

144

Introducing sweet Romeo, dear long-haired black German Shepherd rescue and famous runaway

Rio likes to sleep upside down against a wall, with his front paws wrapped around the doorway. He's a sweet upside down pup cake!

Rio celebrating Valentine's Day with Mum and posing for a photo

Rio flirting sweetly with one of his many girlfriends, always a gentleman, offering his paw gently to her and asking, "Would you be my friend and come play with me?"

Rio celebrating his WCRL rally tournament ribbons and 2018 year-end top Veteran ranking

Rio posing for Mum with his first WCRL Rally High Combined win ribbon!

Rio relaxing at the Sandy Hook Gateway National Recreation
Area, watching the shore birds and enjoying the cool breeze

Rio enjoying a day at Sandy Hook

Rio posing at a dog trial at Kellar's Canine Academy

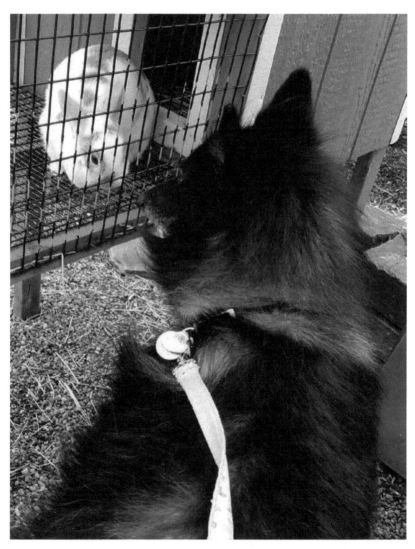

Rio saying "hello" to his new friend, a bunny rabbit

*Handsome Rio, with his perfect score medal at Kellar's
Canine Academy*

Rio posing with his WCRL RLVX24 title, High-Combined Ribbons, Perfect Score and placement ribbons after trials at Golden Rule School for Dogs

CHAPTER 28

Run for the Door

"No one saves us but ourselves. No one can and no one may. We ourselves must walk the path."

—*Buddha*

omeo's first training class was an introductory obedience class at St. Hubert's Dog Training School. He learned the commands quickly at home, being a very smart Shepherd. He is so smart he often anticipates what I want him to do.

When we were in class, it was a different story. He was very nervous, and it was clear that his main goal was to get out of the building and run away. It was just too much pressure for him.

Whenever Romeo entered an unfamiliar room, he seemed to take notice of where the doors were located. Romeo always seemed to keep one eye on the door, so I developed a concern that he may run for the door at some point and try to escape. I also had a strong feeling that this highly intelligent dog could figure out how to push the door open.

One day in class, we were practicing a recall, front, around, and side. I directed Romeo to do so and he did exactly what I asked of him, ending up in a nice sit at my left side. But after sitting, he looked at me with a frightened look in his eyes, telling me, "Sorry Mum, I have had enough of this," whereupon he ran at full speed across the room for the door.

He was so stressed, and I felt so bad for him. This was just too much for him.

My heart broke for Romeo, as did everyone's in our class.

How could someone take the responsibility of breeding dogs so lightly — by not socializing them properly and creating such a fearful dog? Even if a breeder was not going to show this dog, they should have socialized him. They brought him into this world, it was not his choice to be here. How could they be so cruel?

Our instructor recommended we try a class for aggressive dogs and dogs with issues. Romeo did very well in the class and did not have a problem with anxiety toward other dogs. Dogs were not the problem. Rather, Romeo was mostly concerned about being in places with which he was unfamiliar.

We also took Romeo to be evaluated by Pia at St. Hubert's, a certified professional dog trainer and canine behavior consultant. We sat with Pia, and for over an hour we let Romeo roam freely to explore the room. Romeo paced nervously around the room at first, then he went under the table for a while. He finally calmed down and approached Pia.

At the end of the session, Pia confirmed that Romeo is a very sweet boy, but because of his lack of socialization at a very young age, he is afraid of many things most dogs take for granted. She said he is very timid, and it would be good to socialize him as much as we could. The good news was that Romeo is a very smart and very good boy, and he does not have a mean bone in his body.

Pia recommended we sign Romeo up for nose work classes to both socialize him and give him a job to do. I did not know anything about the sport, but we signed Romeo up for the next available class, which happened to be an introductory nose work class.

The goal of the introductory class was to teach our dogs to find a target odor, birch (which was hidden in a box), and to alert us to its location. Romeo learned to find the birch quickly, but doing this in a new location and large class forum proved to be too stressful for him.

Romeo was worried about the location of the other dogs and people in the room and had to figure that out before he did his search. When he did find the scent, he was usually too nervous to take food as a reward. Alternatively, I generously praised him in lieu of food.

I decided for the short term, I would continue his nose work training at home and in private lessons, where he had much better focus and confidence and would take food as a reward. His skills have developed nicely, and he now does very well with nose work searches. His abilities impress me — it is as if he is a police dog on a mission when he is doing a search. Because Romeo enjoys working with his nose, I have expanded his training to tracking and he is doing extremely well.

All this training helped us bond closer and increased Romeo's confidence significantly. It took time, but Romeo learned he could trust me and that I was not going to hurt him. At home, Romeo became such a different dog, very self-assured and a very good family dog, watch dog, and our very good friend.

He does well at everything I introduce him to, once he gets past his fears. He is a very smart boy, so

I decided to train him for the American Kennel Club Canine Good Citizen test. With consistent positive training and continued socialization, I was thrilled that Romeo passed the test on his first try. Positive training and love pay off!

CHAPTER 29

Veteran

"Persist, don't quit ... just keep trying and success
will smile upon you!"

—*Joni*

Time flew by quickly, and we returned to rally
before we knew it. Rio turned seven years old,
making him a Veteran in the World Cynosport
Rally world, per their requirements at the time. I decided
we would return, to see what rally moves we both had
left in us.

Rio loved being back in the ring. The Veterans class
was still competitive, at times very much so, with some
fantastic dogs in the class, but didn't have as many signs
as the other levels. There are about 12 signs allowed,
chosen from a more limited universe of signs. Some of
the more challenging signs such as jumps are excluded
for Veterans, and sits and downs are limited because a
lot of sits and downs can be hard on an older dog's body.
We have enjoyed these trials and have had some very

memorable moments while earning some lovely colorful ribbons.

When Rio earned his Rally Veteran Title, he also earned an "Award of Excellence — Veteran" for earning all of his scores above 190 points. After earning the Rally Veteran title, Rio became eligible to work toward various levels of Veteran Championships. With each new set of five qualifying scores, a Veteran earns another Championship title.

Later that spring, Rio and I trialed at the Golden Rule School For Dogs in Andover, New Jersey. We showed in Veterans, and there were six competitors: one in Level A (seeking the Veteran's title); five in Level B (already having earned the Veteran's title, but now working on various Championships).

We arrived early, and I walked Rio around for a while to get him acclimated to the site, as we had not been there in a couple of years. He found the site very interesting, with lots of trees and bushes containing very interesting scents, so he sniffed for about 10 minutes, focusing on every scent he could find.

Puppies ran first, and they had just started their first trial. The puppies were scheduled to run both of their trials first, back to back, then Veterans would go next and run both of their trials back to back as well. There were only a couple of puppy entries, so their runs and ribboning went very quickly.

I love (as do others) when the trials are scheduled this way because, after your final run, you can pack up and leave to start the rest of the day. This is much easier on the Veteran dogs who often tire more easily and get tired waiting at a trial all day for a second run. Some trials are run with a trial in the morning and a second in the afternoon, so it can take up an entire day for two trials, which can be a very long day for a Veteran.

I checked in and found the course maps for Veteran trials one and two. A course map is a map of the course layout and shows the signs that will be used in that run. Competitors should review each course map ahead of the course walk-through to familiarize themselves with the course.

Both Veteran courses were constructed to move quickly and without a lot of sits. I studied the map for trial one and walked the course a few times with the other competitors, then went outside to get Rio. He was second in the running order, so we had to hurry. Because the course was very fast, by the time we could get back into the building, a friend was already calling for me to hurry — the judge was ready for Rio.

We hurried into the building and went right into the ring.

"Start when you are ready," the judge instructed.

"Thank you," I replied, then I turned to Rio, smiled, and said cheerfully to my best friend, "It's Showtime buddy, let's go for a walk." And off we went.

The first sign was a Call Front Finish Right, then a Sit Walk Around, then a Left Turn, Serpentine Weave, Left Turn, 360 Degree Right Turn, Left About Turn, then a Moving Stand Leave Dog and Call to Heel, then a Left Turn, Moving Sidestep Right, About Right Turn, and for the bonus, Halt Leave Dog and Call to Heel, then the Finish. If you don't know what any of this means, please look it up online in the rules on the World Cynosport Rally website, I have a feeling you'll be amazed by what people and their beloved dogs can do.

Rio heeled nicely and did everything I asked. The judge said Rio did a nice job, and we exited the ring. The other four dogs finished up quickly, then ribbons were awarded. Jen and her handsome black Belgian Sheepdog Seeker finished with a perfect 210 score in first place, Liz and her beautiful Tervuren Ace finished in second place with a perfect 210, but at a slightly slower speed, and we finished with a 209 in third place. What a marvelous job Rio had done!

A talented group, was it not? And we all had a wonderful time having fun showing our dear old Veteran pup friends and playing with them in the ring.

The judge called us into the ring to do the walkthrough for the second course. We walked the course, then it was our turn in the ring. Like run one, run two was a quick course. It felt like Rio did another nice job, and the judge complimented Rio on a very nice run. I praised Rio excitedly.

The other competitors ran the course, then the qualifying dogs were ribboned. Seeker earned first place with a perfect 210 score, Ace earned second place with a score of 209, and Rio earned third place with a score of 208. Again, very good scores for all. We all were thrilled!

Rio and I looked forward to our next show weekend in June at the World Cynosport Rally trials at Kellar's in Saddlebrook, New Jersey. We very much enjoyed seeing old friends and meeting new ones. Rio was again a hard worker that weekend and earned his first Rally Veteran Championship. I hugged him and cried, so grateful we were together and that he did so well. He always was, and always will be, my star.

In the summer of 2017, Kellar's held its annual World Cynosport Rally Tournament. I entered Rio in the Veteran trials both days, three back-to-back runs each morning. Rio ran very nicely, earning his Rally Veteran Championship Two.

Rio was awarded large rosettes for all six of his placements, as well as a magnificent rosette for his Championship title. Additionally, his scores were very nice — a perfect 210, two 208s, a 206, a 205 and a 201.

Thank you judges and Kellar's for the titles and beautiful ribbons! It means so much to me because Rio is older, and these may be some of his final runs. I will treasure them forever.

Later that summer, Rio and I trialed again in Andover. There were two trials that day, with six Veterans entered in the first trial, four in the second. I was very tired because I could not sleep much the night before from excitement about the show. I got up 4:30 a.m. to eat breakfast, then feed and brush Rio and ready everything for the car. Rio slept well and was ready to go, always in the mood to sniff and flirt with the other dogs.

The show ran efficiently, with volunteers changing ring signs while the class who ran before were being ribboned, so the ring was ready for us in no time. We were third in the run order, and I could see the course would move quickly as it did not require a lot of sits and downs. As usual, I had my show nerves. We walked up to the Start sign and the judge instructed us to go when ready.

"Ready! Let's go for a walk buddy!" I said to Rio.

Off we went to the first sign, Moving Side Step Right, then Call Front Finish Left, Sit Down Walk Around, Right Turn, Serpentine Weave Once, Right Turn, About Turn Right, About U Turn, Slow Pace, Normal Pace, Halt Sit, Halt Sit Stand, then for the bonus, Turn and Down, then the Finish.

"Good boy, Rio! I love you, sweetie!" I excitedly praised him when we were done. He was simply wonderful.

"Nice job!" the judge said. I thought we had a nice run, but I never know exactly how well until we see the final score. We exited the ring, and I walked Rio around outside to relieve himself and have fun.

"Go sniff!"

Sniffing is a favorite pastime for him and often a reward he loves. It is a work of art for him. Sometimes he sniffs with such focus and intensity it's like he is trying to determine an elusive bitch's DNA.

We returned inside the building and heard the judge call, "All Veterans enter the ring for ribboning!"

On the way into the ring, I glanced at the roster where the stewards list the run order of dogs and add their scores after their runs. I looked and it seemed to say 205 by Rio's name. I blinked and double checked. Rio ran third today, not fourth. He earned a perfect score of 210!

The judge awarded ribbons and we were elated to receive a stunning striped rosette — red and white — for second place. Rio had a perfect score but came in second place due to time, being only seconds slower than the other dog. How proud I am of my Rio!

Our second run was very nice, a similar course with a few sign changes, so it ran quickly. I thought that we had at least one minor flaw with our performance, so I was thrilled that we received a score of 208 and a lovely black and white striped fourth place ribbon.

Go, Rio! What a grand day!

We trialed at about a dozen show weekends that year at different locations in New Jersey and Pennsylvania. Rio had a very good year, earning a number of Veteran Championship titles, plus his first High Combined award for the highest average of all Veterans at two trials at Andover. We had never earned a High Combined award before, so that rosette is extra special!

I was elated when I saw the World Cynosport Rally National Rankings for end of year 2017. Rio ranked third in the Veteran Championship class, both in the United States and the World. We continued to trial in 2018, and to my surprise and joy, Rio placed first in the Veteran Championship class in the 2018 National Rankings and in the World!

Recently, Rio and I had a dream weekend at Andover. He earned his 24th Veteran Championship (RLVX24), two High Combined ribbons, along with top placements and perfect scores. This means so much to me. I believe that our teamwork has improved as our ever-deepening relationship and increasing communications have blossomed over time.

We have also started participating with Cyber-Rally O, an online venue, where you can do their rally courses at your leisure and locations of your choice and not have to wait or travel an hour or two to a trial. You can even do the rally courses in your own backyard. I love playing rally with Rio, and I want to keep him happy and active, so whatever Rio wants — to go out to trials or stay home — it shall be.

As long as Rio wants to get out and do rally, I will be there by his side. Rio moves around the course a little slower than years ago, which makes me so sad. I usually tear up at each trial with the realization that my Rio is now a Veteran nearing the autumn of his life. I will rally with Rio until he is bored of it and does not want to do it anymore.

CHAPTER 30

Meet the Breeds

*"Magic is in the air … come meet the Belgian dogs
and the other breeds!"*

—*Joni*

Our first journey to Westminster in New York City in 2015 was not for the conformation show, but for the Meet the Breeds Event the Westminster Dog Show had added on the Saturday before the conformation show at the Piers.

At Meet the Breeds, dog owners exhibit their dogs and educational materials for the joy and education of the public. People are encouraged to meet and play with dogs representing more than 100 different breeds, and to ask their owners questions to see if that breed is well suited for them and their families. The AKC recently added cats to the Meet the Breeds event.

Each breed has its own American Kennel Club booth that is decorated by the breed club and its members to represent something special about the breed. This could be, among other things, the breed's nation of origin, history of the breed, and their talents and historical uses, e.g. herding, sporting, and working breeds. The enthusiastic and very professional breed club members have continued to decorate their booths in increasingly spectacular and creative ways each year, making a visit to the show to meet their dogs and learn about their breed truly an awesome and memorable experience.

Months before the first Meet the Breeds event at the Piers, the American Belgian Tervuren Club reached out to its membership for volunteers to assist at the event, so Rio and I volunteered. Sally, a member of the club, volunteered to head up the team comprised of other members including Elizabeth, Erika, Joelle, Patti, and me, and best of all, our beloved Tervuren.

It was a wonderful day — Valentine's Day. Love was in the air, and petting and hugs for the dogs were many, despite the very cold weather and snow.

The event was crowded within moments of the doors opening. Families and friends came to enjoy the event, despite the inclement weather, all looking excitedly for their favorite dogs and to meet new breeds of interest!

We had many hundreds, perhaps thousands, of visitors at our booth. Most people seemed new to the Tervuren breed and were anxious to see them and find out more information about them. Most of our dogs were exhibited on the grooming tables, enabling an eye-level view for passers-by. Rio stood happily on the floor, mingling with the visitors.

People asked many questions about our dogs and the Tervuren breed. So many enjoyed the breed's beauty, sense of humor, intelligence, and exceptional temperaments. They were impressed by the Tervuren's quick learning skills and ability to perform so many diverse activities, from their long-time war and police dog roles, their historic herding role, to therapy and service dog work, excelling at all types of performance sports like agility and obedience, and simply being excellent family members and best friends.

Our dogs were remarkable with the children, who enthusiastically engaged with our pups, petting and hugging them, and watching our dogs play together during the day. Many a photo was taken with a joyful child.

Rio was a marvelous ambassador of the breed, and many people loved to pet him and find out more about him and his breed. He proudly wore his Dog Scout of America bandana (he had become a member recently), and many inquired about the organization. We made a quick visit to the Girl Scouts of America booth, and the Girl Scouts enjoyed interacting with Rio and the fact that Rio was also a Scout!

I later decorated Rio with little Valentine stickers on his harness. More love was in the air! Rio enjoyed flirting with the other dogs and held his own "Meet and Greet Rio."

Since that wonderful day, our American Belgian Tervuren Club team and our dogs have returned every year to the Meet the Breeds event. We take educational materials, along with Valentine's Day and other decorations to enhance the Belgian exhibit for the event. Large heart decorations, white holiday lights to adorn the top of the backdrop wall, a digital picture viewer to show pictures of our dogs in action, and last but not least, a life-size stuffed-toy sheep. It is fun to bring my pretty ewe to represent our breed's sheep herding history, and children and adults of all ages are drawn to her to have their photos taken with her.

But best of all, and the center of attention, are our Belgian Tervuren. Each of our Tervs has a unique personality, but all are well-behaved, proudly representing the breed, and get all the attention — including having lots of photos and selfies taken with the visitors. It is a magnificent event and an honor to participate in it.

Every year, Meet the Breeds has been a joyful day, both for the visitors, our dogs, and us — the exhibitors. To our surprise and delight, in 2017 a well-known television reporter, Rachel Bonnetta, stopped by to talk to the sheep. A video of this conversation was included in that Monday's Westminster Dog Show television coverage. Joe was surprised while watching the show to see the sheep on television.

On arriving home that day, I was thrilled to see posted on Facebook an announcement that our Tervuren booth was awarded "First Place - Herding Group," based on creativity, the dogs, and friendliness of the owners.

We had very full hearts, so very proud of our beloved companion and best friend Rio, and how he made so many people happy, as he makes us every day. We were so proud to share him with the public as a representative of his breed, with all the other beloved Tervuren and their loving owners. What a wonderful finish to the day!

CHAPTER 31

National to Westminster

"Aim high, shoot for the stars, try hard and you will always succeed in life my friend. It's not always about the result, but the enjoyable ride on the way."

—*Joni*

For our next adventure, Rio and I were excited to be traveling to our first Belgian Tervuren National in Gettysburg, Pennsylvania, a three-hour drive from home. It was wonderful to be with so many American Belgian Tervuren Club members and their beautiful dogs, and it turned out to be a wonderful and very rewarding experience for us.

At the National, a once-a-year gathering of Tervuren and their owners from all around the United States, there were conformation shows as well as rally, obedience, herding, and agility trials. We met hundreds of wonderful Tervuren owners and their dogs. Rio had already finished competing in American Kennel Club rally (having completed his AKC Rally Advanced Excellent title, the highest American Kennel Club title at the time) and conformation, and we were not ready for the obedience, herding, or tracking trials, so we did not compete in any of the events.

Instead, we met up with many old friends, made a lot of new friends, both human and canine, and shared lots of stories and camaraderie, as well as cheers when they earned a qualifying score (leg) or title. Rio was in heaven, with dozens of Terv girlfriends flirting with him and begging for his attention.

We enjoyed every bit of it — the team obedience I had never seen before, the honor parade that commemorates older dogs for certain accomplishments, but most of all, all the gorgeous dogs.

We enjoyed participating in the Terv Two-Miler Hike early in the morning one day. We also participated in lighting candles at night in remembrance of past dogs and in celebration of current ones, a heartwarming event. I lit a candle marked with the phrase I had written on it, "Rio — you light up my life."

As part of the wonderful experience, the club offered the new American Kennel Club Urban Canine Good Citizen title test. I signed Rio up and he was a star, passing it nicely. We were so happy to receive this new title.

It was a fun week and went so fast. It was Terv heaven on earth for Rio. He looked at me, grinning, on the last day and said, "Mum, this just cannot get any better!" Rio was sad to have the week end and asked me, "Mum, when can we come back?"

Thank you, American Belgian Tervuren Club, for such a fun time and fantastic memories!

∞

Not long after, I decided we were going to show at Westminster!

Although I am a new handler and Rio is my first show dog, I had dreamed of showing him at Westminster from the moment I started taking conformation classes with him. The Westminster Dog Show is a fantastic, prestigious show with so much glorious history and top dogs representing their breeds. It is a great honor to be there and participate in the event.

Rio had earned his Championship and so he well met the requirements for entry to the show. As such, I entered him (with a lot of excitement!) into the 140th Annual Westminster Kennel Club Dog Show.

We had enjoyed participating in Meet the Breeds at the Piers the Saturday before, so I felt a lot of excitement building in anticipation of the show on Monday. Sunday came quickly, and I started getting very nervous. The show was tomorrow! I anxiously packed up my car on Sunday night.

When I awoke at 4 a.m. on Monday with butterflies in my stomach, I whispered to Rio, "Rio, it is Showtime today. Time to go see your girlfriends!" Rio jumped up, grinning, with his tail wagging. He was ready to go. Rio did not mind getting up early, eating an early breakfast, and getting into the car. My good friend, Geri, was glad to join me and help out. We arrived, set up in the benching area and waited for the show to begin.

The Tervuren were scheduled to show early. The time arrived and Rio and I went ringside, where we anxiously waited to be called in. Many of the country's top ranked Tervuren were there — right beside us. How exciting and what a thrill this was!

The Tervuren were called into the ring. We went around the ring with the other dogs, stacked, did our out-and-back, and around. Rio did all I could ask of him, and I was very proud.

After all was said and done, we did not win anything. The dogs in the ring with us were some of the best, with very experienced handlers who have been showing top dogs for many years. It was an honor to meet them and just be in the ring with them, with my Champion Rio, even if just once. Rio put on a good show both in and out of the ring. Outside the ring he was a star. He makes new friends quickly, and he had a lot of old and new fans cheering for him, and that warmed my heart.

Westminster is a benched show, a show where the dogs are given a bench where they are on display throughout the day so that spectators can stop and interact with the dogs and speak with their owners. We spent most of our time at the benching area, hanging out with the other Tervs and handlers in our assigned area. It was fun talking with them and sharing stories. Many hundreds of people stopped by to admire our beautiful Tervs.

Rio enjoyed every minute of the show, happily greeting all the dogs who passed by and flirting with old and new girlfriends. I have photos of Rio at the show as well as some memorabilia, and will treasure that day always. It was truly a grand day!

CHAPTER 32

Are You Obedient?

*"Practice, practice and practice some more — it will
all come together!"*

—Joni

The dogs and handlers who compete in obedience trials are so impressive! Some teams are so incredibly focused and perfect in execution. I love watching their impeccable teamwork.

I hoped that by taking obedience lessons, Rio and I would have a closer relationship and improved teamwork and become more like those awesome teams. I decided to take a few lessons with Rio to see how he would do, despite him not being food or toy driven, and signed Rio up with some of the best trainers.

Our first lessons were group lessons with a very accomplished trainer who often earns high scores in trials with her dogs. We trained for about six months and learned a lot, but made it just halfway through the class schedule, at which time I decided to stop because we were not progressing enough. Rio was very good with much of the training, he loved jumping, did solid sits, downs, and stays most of the time, and was okay with heeling. As such, we loved all of our obedience classes — until we got to the "go-outs" and "retrieves."

The first big challenge was that Rio was just not interested in food, even though we were in evening classes, and he had not eaten since breakfast and was surely hungry.

One exercise that challenged us was the "go-out" exercise, where the handler teaches the dog on command to leave the handler and run to the opposite side of the ring, where the dog will turn around to face the handler, sit, then await further commands from the handler. The instructor trained the go-outs by spraying some string cheese onto a stanchion (an upright post that holds up the ring gates). Most dogs left their handlers with much joy and high speed to get the cheese. Rio was the exception.

It turned out Rio's lack of interest in string cheese (or any other food, for that matter) did not get him running, or even walking, to the stanchion. He did saunter over to the stanchion a couple of times to see what the other dogs found so exciting, but when he arrived merely sniffed the cheese curiously and appeared to think, "What's the big deal?" then walked away, finding sniffing the ground for dog scents much more interesting.

Frustrating for both me and our instructors alike, and despite my best efforts, Rio is not consistently food-driven. This results in him not being as driven as other dogs in many ways. His heeling is not as close and crisp as other dogs, he does not move as quickly, and he has no use for cheese on stanchions for go-outs.

As he was not food-driven when we got him, I have worked hard to increase his food drive. With much effort and lots of training, and trying nearly every treat I could think of, I have made some progress in improving his food drive, but it still is neither strong nor consistent.

At home, there are times Rio is hungry enough and wants the food, so he heels perfectly. But in the ring, where the excitement of a show and other dogs takes over, the promise of a treat at the end of the performance is not important to Rio, and his heeling varies from nice to lagging feet behind me. As I mentioned earlier, Rio is not interested in toys, either.

Our obedience instructor had another technique beyond food and toys to teach the retrieve. She used an ear pinch to encourage dogs to take the retrieve object. I watched her do that to one dog in the class, and thought I could never do it to Rio, as he is extremely sensitive, probably more than most dogs, and I believed it would hurt him.

When it was our turn in class, I pressed Rio's ear between my two fingers very lightly, applying hardly any pressure. After his response, we were done with that. Let me be clear — I did not pinch Rio's ear, I just did a gentle press, yet Rio backed away and looked at me beseechingly with his gentle brown eyes, very concerned, saying, "Mum, I love you. Why are you hurting me?"

I felt his pain. After Rio's expressive response, I immediately decided I would never use the ear pinch or press, even if it means we could never compete in obedience. It is not worth it. His love means more to me than any ribbon or title. Not having success with the go-outs and now the retrieves, I thanked our obedience instructor profusely for all of her top notch training and went on our way.

Though it was difficult to do, I faced the facts: we were obedience school dropouts. But I would not give up. Sometime later, I discovered that a local rally instructor, Linda, was also a very accomplished trainer of obedience.

Her students love her classes, sense of humor, and her utmost patience with silly students. We had fun in her classes, but I think we may have given her a few gray hairs due to Rio's lack of food interest, slow heeling, sniffing, and no retrieves. We took a number of classes and practiced a lot, but after some time and frustration, and limited funding, we took a break from obedience lessons altogether.

But my desire to earn a couple of obedience titles with Rio did not go away, so after a short break, I decided to do what I could on my — our — own. I had learned a lot of the critical obedience basics from our first instructor and Linda, and I believed it was enough to train Rio at home on the basics needed for the American Kennel Club Beginner Novice title.

I practiced and practiced with Rio, a few minutes in the morning, then again, a few minutes at night when I returned home from work. I discovered that if I kept the training sessions short, and focused on just one or two things each time, Rio remained interested.

We began to make good progress, though it was often little steps. With each lesson, I built on each little step of progress.

As I am quickly impatient, and Rio gets bored quickly, I soon decided to give competition a try, entering a number of American Kennel Club trials. To my utmost surprise and joy, Rio earned his American Kennel Club Beginner Novice (BN) title with three first-place ribbons and with decent scores too, though not perfect. As the saying goes, we were not going to let "perfect" become the enemy of the "good."

The next obedience title for Rio was the American Kennel Club Pre-Companion Dog (PCD). Again, we practiced in our yard with treats when he wanted them, and with extra love and lots of praise when he did not want them. Back into the competition ring we went, and Rio earned his PCD title with three first-place ribbons, though again no perfect scores. I was so happy for my boy!

We next practiced for the American Kennel Club Companion Dog (CD) title, working at home a little bit each day. For one of our entries, I signed Rio up for a Belgian Tervuren Specialty in Massachusetts. What an honor it would be to earn a ribbon at the Specialty. Well, we were never destined for their beautiful ribbons or for greatness in any show world, but we sure did have fun and interesting times trying!

We arrived at the show and met a lot of very nice Tervuren owners, chatted and had a great time, but all along I was nervous about entering the ring.

Finally, the show started. Class after class went, then suddenly, it was our turn to enter the ring.

Rio did a good job of heeling on and off lead, the figure eight, and almost everything else. Also entered in the competition was a bitch Rio really likes, one of his many girlfriends, so it was only the two of them in the ring. Time came to do the Sit Stay, which is where you leave your dog in a sit while you walk across to the other side of the ring and remain, until the judge tells you to return to your dog, generally about a minute.

Rio and his girlfriend were both doing a super job in the stay. Each second went very slowly, one breath seeming like an eternity. Finally, the time was almost up, Rio might qualify!

With only about twenty seconds left in the stay, for no apparent reason, Rio's girlfriend went into a down. She was disqualified, but Rio stayed in his sit!

I watched Rio so closely, praying he would remain in the sit-stay. It was so difficult, because I could not say anything to Rio, I could not tell him he was a good boy or what a magnificent job he was doing and to just stay where he was!

Ten seconds left...

Suddenly, Rio turned to look at his girlfriend who had gone into a down.

To my utter amazement, Rio quickly looked around, the expression on his face suggesting he thought, "Oh no, I missed the command. Mum will be upset." He looked at me briefly, then immediately dropped into a down position ... just seconds before he would have qualified!

We were so close — I could not believe Rio had just NQ'd!

I was stunned, but I smiled, and both the judge and I looked at Rio, laughed, and asked, "Rio, what was that all about, little man?"

Rio was trying to be such a good boy, so I could not be disappointed with him. He only wanted to please me, and that was worth everything, more than a ribbon. We were just not meant for the big Specialty world.

We anxiously waited for the next show in Oaks, Pennsylvania. Rio qualified! We were thrilled to complete Rio's CD title, not with top scores, but with three more first-place ribbons! It was a beautiful touch that Santa was there for photos with my happy, charming boy. Rio knew he did well and had a smile on his face and a prance in his walk. He was clearly very proud.

Before we can enter the next level, Rio must know how to retrieve, so as part of our training both in class and at home, we are starting to once again work on retrieves, using positive dog training and positive rewards. We also recently decided to give obedience lessons another try and signed up for a few more of Linda's obedience classes after having taken a break. We learn so much from her classes, and on top of that, Rio and I both have so much fun. I enjoy catching up with old friends, and Rio enjoys flirting with his girlfriends, especially Jeanne's pretty German Shepherd gals, Kathy's very attractive young Sheltie, and others.

Rio seems to have girlfriends everywhere he goes. He is such a friendly and charming young man, always filled with joy. He is one of the friendliest Belgian dogs I have ever met. Maybe somehow they can entice him to do a retrieve!

CHAPTER 33

I Herd You!

"Don't ever give up on doing something you want to do! Try again my friend, you shall succeed!"

—*Joni*

As Rio is a Tervuren, a herding breed, I decided it was time to see if he liked herding sheep.

Many Tervuren have good herding instincts and have the daily job of herding sheep or ducks on their own farm. For those not so lucky to live on a farm, there are herding trials in a number of venues where Tervuren can show off their herding prowess with sheep, ducks, and if so skilled, cattle.

I searched online for herding lessons and discovered the Raspberry Ridge Sheep Farm in Pennsylvania, about an hour and a half away. They were having a herding instinct test in a few weeks, so I signed Rio up and off we went.

The sheep farm is beautiful, with lovely hills and trees, and Rio and I love it there. The instinct test included a dozen or so sheep contained securely in a large pen. Rio and I were instructed to stay outside the pen, but I was told to let Rio approach the fence and allow him to enjoy the sheep. I was instructed not to stop him from chasing them. After all, they were in the pen, and he was outside of it and could not harm them.

I followed the instructions of the evaluator and owner of the farm, Carolyn. Rio was on a long line lead, and was very engaged with the sheep, following their every move. At one point, apparently comfortable with Rio's disposition, Carolyn told me to let Rio off his lead. He was free to do what he wanted on the outside of the pen. Rio ran back and forth from left to right outside the ring, trying to find a way to get to the sheep. He could not reach the sheep because the fence was between them and the gate was closed.

After a few minutes of observing Rio's behavior, Carolyn wrote an assessment. She gave Rio a passing grade on the instinct test and had very positive comments about his temperament with the sheep.

Our herding adventure began!

I signed up for a couple of Carolyn's herding seminars, where I learned a lot about sheep herding theory, then Rio and I were able to practice with the sheep. Rio loved the sheep and wanted to chase them, but that was not what was supposed to be happening. Rather, he was supposed to learn to steadily guide the sheep as I, the shepherd, instructed him in a calm manner.

Poor Rio! I did not know what to do, and poor Rio was looking up to me for guidance that just was not there! I listened to Carolyn's instructions, but usually reacted much too slowly to have any effect on Rio or the sheep.

Not one to give up easily, I bought some herding books to learn more about what we were supposed to be doing. Hmmm....

My reading confirmed, as I had already guessed, that herding is one of the most difficult dog sports. Not only must I know what to do to control my dog, but I must be able to read the actions of the sheep and anticipate what they are going to do. My actions must help my dog control the sheep, and the dog must be able to keep control of the sheep and move them to me, even if the dog cannot hear or see me.

In herding trials there are obstacles involved, around or through which a dog has to move the sheep. Some dogs also can effectively use their instinct, initiative, and their own judgment to herd the sheep, without much guidance from their shepherd. There are standard commands handlers generally learn and teach their dogs, which I'd been introduced to in the herding seminars:

"Come by" — Generally, this means to go around the sheep in a clockwise direction.

"Away to me" — Generally, this means to go around the sheep in a counterclockwise direction.

"Walk up" — Tells the dog to slowly move straight at the sheep.

"Look back" — This means the dog should look behind him/her for more sheep.

"That'll do" — Tells the dog to stop and come back to its handler.

There are many other commands, and in addition, many handlers use a whistle instead of verbal commands. Using a whistle comes in handy, especially when the sheep and dog are far away from the handler or behind a hill or trees, as the dog may not hear the handler's voice or see her/him.

We took many fun lessons with Carolyn, then we were referred to Gene, a very accomplished competitor in herding trials with top-notch working Border Collies on a farm much closer to us. With his guidance, we gained the skills and confidence to start competing in the American

Kennel Club and American Herding Breed Association venues.

Gene and his wife Teri have a lovely farm with sheep, ducks, geese, chickens, pigs, and horses. Gene herds with his Border Collies, and has several Maremma sheepdogs who guard his sheep. Gene does a nice job training the handlers of various herding breeds to work with their dogs, and adapts the training to the needs of each breed and each dog.

I have taken both Rio and Romeo to train with Gene. We trained with Gene for several months, and then, with his encouragement, I signed Rio up for the herding capability tests. I thought he was ready.

Our first test, the American Herding Breed Association Herding Capability Test, was at the lovely Fly Away Farm in Pennsylvania. To earn this title, we had to pass a two-part test. It is a pass/fail test.

The requirement of the first leg of the test was for the dog to demonstrate a good stop and a recall with sheep in the ring. The second part was to hold a pause before the dog gathered the sheep, then move the sheep across the ring with a change in direction, before the dog is told to stop and is recalled.

Rio was frisky that day, being at a farm he had never visited before with new sheep friends. Despite this, he did a very nice job and earned his American Herding Breed Association Herding Capability Tested title with sheep (HCT-s). I was thrilled!

Later that month, we earned Rio's American Kennel Club Herding Test title. Another pass/fail test, we were required to earn two qualifying runs to earn the title. Rio had to move the sheep across the ring between two cones, three times. Also required were a stop and a recall at the end of the test. We had 10 minutes to complete the test.

The first time we took this test it was a bit trying, as I did not yet have a stock stick and Rio cheerfully ran around the sheep part of the time. However, Rio completed all the requirements and earned the first leg. The second time we took the test at a different farm. Again, Rio was frisky, but he moved the sheep and met all the test requirements. And he earned two pretty rosettes for his efforts!

We then started working toward earning Rio's American Herding Breed Association Junior Herding Dog Test title (JHD). To pass the test, we had to qualify in two runs under different judges. We entered two tests at Fly Away Farm held by two different judges. For each test, two panels with a 12-foot opening between them were set up side-by-side in the center of the ring. Two additional panels were set up, one at each of the farthest corners of the ring, each parallel to and 12-feet from the fence.

Three sheep were used for each test, placed in the ring well off the fence not too far from the entrance gate of the ring.

For the first test, I brought Rio into the ring on leash, then the judge instructed me to remove his leash. Rio held the stay. Then I went through the center panels, with Rio confidently moving the sheep through the panels behind me, then he moved the sheep between the fence and far panel on the left, along the fence to the right, and between the fence and far panel on the right. Rio then guided the sheep to the pen, and held them in place. I opened the gate, in the sheep went, and I closed the gate. Rio waited calmly outside the pen. We redid the course later under a different judge, and qualified in both instances, earning Rio's Junior Herding Dog Title (JHD-s) and two very nice rosettes for our memories. A wonderful day!

We had a more challenging time earning Rio's American Kennel Club Pre-Trial herding test title. To qualify, he had to pass the test twice. The test included a controlled pause or stay by the dog at the beginning of the test; controlled passage of sheep around the ring, clearing two gates; doing one stop of the sheep on the course; reversing the direction of the sheep; clearing the two gates in the opposite direction, and stopping the sheep and your dog while you open the gate to release the sheep and pen them. This all must be completed in 10 minutes.

We took the tests at the lovely Scarlet Mill Farm in Pennsylvania under different judges. The first trial was not only very interesting as our first attempt at this test, but it was also very memorable. A day or so before the trial, an unusually heavy storm had flooded the trial field. The result was very thick, gooey mud, maybe four to five inches deep in spots.

As a result, while leading the sheep and Rio through the course, both of my shoes came off in the mud!

What was this girl to do? Get my shoes or finish the course?

I knew we had practiced too hard to give up on the course, so I continued without shoes — only with my socks with little white sheep figures on them that I had worn for good luck. A day I will never forget! Nothing is simple for us!

Despite the challenges, we qualified at our next trial. We were nervous entering the ring, but Judge Pritchard was very supportive. He asked if we had ever tried this before, to which I replied, "Yes, but we NQ'd."

He inquired as to what happened, then encouraged us at every step of the test, saying, "You are doing good!" and, "Keep moving!" I guess he could see that sometimes I overthink things and get caught up in my shoestrings. With his encouragement, Rio and I completed the course successfully and qualified in about two minutes and thirty-five seconds. I gained a lot of confidence that day.

Our next run was at Scarlet Mill Farm a couple of weeks later, before another judge. I felt confident, and Rio sensed that. This run went very smoothly in comparison to our earlier ones. Our run went so smoothly, in fact, that the judge did not seem to think Rio was working hard enough! Rio was indeed moving the sheep, albeit without the circling and excited movement exhibited by some breeds.

Afterward, while awarding the ribbons, the judge emphasized that all breeds are different and handle sheep in different ways. And that was how Rio finished his American Kennel Club PT title.

We are currently training for the next American Kennel Club level, Herding Started, but in the meantime we were happy to discover a new title was being offered by the American Kennel Club, the Farm Dog Certified Test. We could not wait to try it, so signed up for the first event in our area.

CHAPTER 34

Farm Dog!

"How fun and exciting it is to try new things!"

—Joni

The first Farm Dog Certified Test in our area was in Windsor, New York, hosted by the Susque-Nango Kennel Club. The goal of the Farm Dog Certified Test is to test a dog in situations that she or he may encounter in an actual farm environment. Some of the traits the evaluated dog must exhibit are confidence and self-control in a farm environment with farm animals.

The requirements of the American Kennel Club test were:

1. Greet the Evaluator — Initial Dog Appraisal.

2. Perform a Walk Pattern Around Farm Environment and By Passive Stranger.

3. Jump on Hay/Straw Bale.

4. Walk by Farm Animal(s).

5. Walk Over or Through Unusual Surfaces.

6. Supervised Separation.

7. Pass Through a Gate.

8. Handler Feeds Livestock.

9. Reaction to Another Dog.

10. Reaction to Noise Distraction.

11. Dog Approaches Livestock.

12. Physical Examination.

I was nervous about the test because Rio does not like being put in a crate, which is a requirement. Since the day he came to live with us, he has acted like I am punishing him whenever I put him in his crate, so I do not put him in there anymore.

But he would have to be crated twice in one day, maybe in a few hours, to pass the Farm Dog Certified Test. Despite the slim chance of this, I decided to drive nearly three hours one way and give the test a go.

It was a long ride, and we got lost for several miles before finally finding the farm where the test was to be held. It was a cozy and beautiful farm, owned by very nice people.

The club representatives running the event were also wonderful people; it was so nice chatting with them during the day. They ran the tests very efficiently and things moved along quickly.

Soon it was our turn. Rio met the judge, and as he is a very well-behaved boy, that went well. Then we walked by livestock and walked a pattern inside a fenced-in area. We then went into a small barn, where Rio had to jump on a hay bale. He did that nicely.

Next was the crate. He had to be crated for a minute or two. As we walked up to the crate, I had no idea if he would do this. I tried to be confident and not let Rio sense my concern that he might not enter the crate, but Rio was confident and went right into the crate.

"Have no worries, Mum!" he said, "I've got you covered!"

Then I had to walk away from Rio for a supervised separation of two minutes. Rio was calm in my absence and had no issues, but was very happy to see me return.

Next, we left the building and walked over the unusual surface (I believe it was a piece of plastic), then off we went into the mud. We went through a gate next, but Rio had to wait until I went through first. Passing farm animals, we then walked to a large barn and entered. I was asked to walk him to the wall, tie his leash to the post and leave him there while I went to feed the livestock about twenty feet away.

Next, I was asked to walk Rio onto a low platform and put him in a stay while another dog walked by, then some participants in the test made a lot of noise to see if Rio had any reaction. He was calm. I next walked him up to a fence, behind which were many sheep. Rio was very well-behaved. The judge then did a physical inspection of Rio, who was calm and friendly. We repeated the same routine again with another judge.

Excellent news — Rio qualified both times! I was so thrilled he had earned his Farm Dog Certification. Rio and I were ecstatic!

After all participants finished the test, we all met to share the lunch the wonderful club provided, delicious homemade food including snacks, salads, burgers, hot dogs, and desserts. It was fabulous! Then the judges awarded gorgeous rosettes. Thank you so much for a beautiful day, everyone!

CHAPTER 35

Boy, Girl, and Dog Scouts

"An awesome way to feel happy and rewarded is to volunteer in your community — community service is wonderful."

—*Joni*

During an Internet search, I discovered the Dog Scouts of America (DSA). I was intrigued; could Rio and I do this?

I learned that, just like the Boy Scouts and the Girl Scouts, this is an organization where responsible scouts are created — but they are dogs! They promote responsible dog ownership and community involvement. The DSA website states its mission as, "To improve the lives of dogs, their owners, and society through humane education, positive training, and community involvement."

To become a Dog Scout, you must video the performance of various obedience behaviors with your dog and submit the videos with your application. Some of the requirements are similar to those of the American

Kennel Club Canine Good Citizen test. As Rio's handler, I had to take a comprehensive written test as well.

It sounded like a wonderful group, so I decided to see if Rio could become a Dog Scout. We put our hearts and souls into this, and Rio was certified as an official Dog Scout of America! I thought that was so cool! And Rio received a Dog Scout badge that I sewed to his new Dog Scout vest.

Since joining, we have had lots of fun doing various activities, many of which are fun sports that earn Dog Scout badges, but also many community-related activities, such as visiting a local nursing home and hospice as a certified therapy dog team as well as cleaning up our neighborhood. There are no Dog Scout troops near us, however, many activities can be done remotely, in some cases by performing certain activities such as therapy dog visits and hikes, and keeping a list of your accomplishments as a team.

To date, Rio has earned his Dog Scout badge, a number of Trail and Pack Dog titles, along with numerous merit badges including his Temperament Test, Therapy Dog 1, Community Service Clean-Up America — Poop, Clean-Up America 2 — Cans/Bottles (two times), Barn Hunt, Rally 1 and Rally 2, and Agility Obstacles 1 badges. We are currently working on other merit badges, including Therapy Dog 2 and Naked Dog Obedience. We earned the Clean-Up America 2 badge two times, which means that, as a team, we have picked up 1,000 bottles and cans in our neighborhood, making it a much cleaner place!

Rio also earned his Community Service 1 badge (another team effort) as I picked up 50 piles of dog poop in our neighborhood left by those dog walkers who do not pick up after their dogs (not a good thing).

Each time Rio has earned a badge, he received a badge along with a congratulatory note that said: "Congratulations! For this award of merit, you can be proud! Whenever you wear it, you'll want to bark right out loud!"

Rio earned his first official title of Trail Dog (TD) when we met the requirements of hiking 50 miles together, including two five-mile checkout hikes. It took many weeks to walk the 50 miles, but it was really fun and good exercise for both of us. Since then, in the last few years, Rio has also earned his Trail Dog Excellent (TDX) title for walking a total of 100 miles, and his Utility Trail Dog Titles UT, UT500, UT750, and UT1000 titles for walking a total of 1,000 miles. We are currently working on finishing the next title.

Rio then earned his Dog Scouts of America Pack Dog (PD) title, "having met the requirements of hiking fifty miles, including a five-mile checkout hike, with the canine carrying all required emergency and survival items." Yes, we hiked all those miles, with Rio wearing his carry vest containing various safety items such as a compass, flashlight, matches, etc.

Thank goodness for Rio and all this exercise, or I would be a bit more voluptuous than I am now. Rio next earned his Dog Scouts of America Pack Dog Excellent. He, "met the requirements of hiking 100 miles, including a 10-mile checkout hike, with the canine carrying all required emergency and survival items." We are now starting on his Utility Pack Dog title, for which we must do another 100 miles including a 10-mile walk!

Just like Boy and Girl Scouts, Rio has a vest on which I sew all the badges he has earned, where they are proudly displayed. I love that Rio is a Dog Scout and am a very proud Dog Scout Mum!

CHAPTER 36

Temperament and Rats

*"Trying new activities can be very rewarding for
anyone at any age."*

—*Joni*

Sometime after the American Kennel Club Urban
CGC test, I noticed the letters "TT" following a
number of dogs' names. Researching the Internet,
I discovered it means "Temperament Tested." This is a
test offered by the American Temperament Test Society,
Inc. (ATTS).

It is a 10-part temperament test, and a very interesting one at that. I signed Rio up for the test in Lancaster,
Pennsylvania. The test, "simulates a casual walk through
a park or neighborhood where everyday life situations
are encountered."

The ATTS website says, "During this walk the dog
experiences visual, auditory and physical stimuli. Neutral,
friendly and threatening situations are encountered,
calling into play the dog's ability to exhibit its ability to

distinguish between non-threatening situations and those calling for more watchful and protective reactions."

The test includes greeting neutral and friendly strangers, reaction to a hidden noise, gunshots, reaction to an opening umbrella, to plastic and wire footing, to a nonthreatening stranger, and to a stranger who appears aggressive.

It is a fun test and very interesting to see how your dog will react. I am accustomed to Rio's behaviors in our neighborhood, but a few of the test situations rarely present themselves to us in our daily life, and others not at all.

Rio was very good during the test, even with his calm response to the gunshots, to which I do not believe he had ever been exposed previously. He was even well-behaved with the aggressive stranger, just looking at him, concerned, but curious as to who this madman in the huge flowing raincoat was.

The most challenging part of the test for Rio was his interaction with the huge umbrella opening right next to him. I never use an umbrella when I walk with him, even in heavier rain, so he is not used to umbrellas. And this was the biggest umbrella I had ever seen! It was no surprise that Rio did not care for it, but to his credit, Rio was neither fearful nor curious about it.

I was delighted Rio passed! Rio was happy to have a fun day out, flirting with many of the other dogs while waiting to take the test, and we were happy to learn that the American Kennel Club now recognizes the Temperament Test for Belgian Tervuren!

∞

Not one to sit still for long, I next discovered the relatively new sport of Barn Hunting, where a maze of straw bales is created, in which rats contained in plastic tubing are hidden in such a way that they are safe and secure from the dogs. Not only must the dog find the rat, but the handler must recognize correctly that the dog found the rat and communicate this to the judge quickly by calling, "Rat!"

In addition, the dog must go through a straw bale tunnel and climb onto a straw bale, all within a limited amount of time. Depending on the level of competition, there may be a different number of rats in the ring. The rats we have worked with are very well-kept family pets who are used to dogs being around them, and the containers keep them safe.

The handler/dog team competes, and as they progress, each level becomes more difficult. The idea of this relatively new sport was derived from the history of some dog breeds who were originally trained to hunt vermin at farms.

We signed up for a training class in East Stroudsburg, Pennsylvania. Rio and I had an excellent training session with Dawn and Robin, who are now Barn Hunt judges. The session started with a short introduction of our dogs to one of their pets, a well-cared for, beautiful white rat.

Everyone in the class then introduced their dogs to the straw bales, encouraging them to climb up on the bales and to go through a tunnel made from many bales. Next, we were introduced to the three-canister system: one containing a rat, one containing used rat bedding with the scent of a rat, and one empty, unused, and unscented container. The dogs were allowed to try to identify the canister containing the rat about four different times.

To my surprise, Rio identified the rat each time! I was the one who had to work hard, trying to figure out from Rio's body language that he had located the rat. One time he wagged his tail at the rat like he was trying to make friends. Other times, Rio kissed the container, pawed it so that it rolled sideways, or just sniffed and sniffed the container. It was clear that once again I had my work cut out for me.

After the preliminary training, we assisted Dawn and Robin in setting up a mock course for a Barn Hunt Instinct Test. This consisted of about 30 or more bales of straw stacked in sections of varying heights, some leaning on others, some forming a tunnel, others placed in the corners of the ring.

The start area was a four-foot wide box-shaped area, marked by four orange mini cones. All dogs and handler teams must stand in the start area until the judge tells them to start, then they have 60 seconds to get to the other end of the ring where the three canisters are placed and identify which one contains the rat. We did this twice.

To my astonishment, for the first run, Rio identified the rat immediately. We ran to the canisters, he sniffed one continuously, and I called out, "Rat!" We did this in four-and-a half seconds! I was stunned, but convinced this was a lucky run. Our next run was slower because Rio decided to sniff the scents on the ground, but still good, 17 seconds! Maybe we were on to something.

Then the ring was reworked for the Novice level competition, a titling event for the Barn Hunt Association that is recognized by the American Kennel Club and United Kennel Club. The canisters were hidden between some of the straw bales, then covered with loose straw so we could not see them. With their amazing scenting ability, the dogs would still be able to smell the rats. In addition to finding the canister with the rat in it, our dogs had to go through the straw bale tunnel, and get up on top of a bale of straw and have all four feet on it. The judge would let us know when we were done.

All this must be done within two minutes!

The ring was ready, and it was our turn. Ready … set … go!

"Tunnel!"

Rio instantly bolted through the tunnel, then veered to the right corner. Sniff-sniff-sniff...

"Rat!" I yelled, and was right!

Then Rio jumped up on to the hay bale, and we were done! It took 37 seconds. Rio took my breath away. I still thought we were just lucky, and wondered if I would always be able to know when Rio found the rat.

The next run started with Rio running right past the tunnel, around the hay bales, then sniff, sniff, sniff ... then he looked at me quizzically, saying, "Well, aren't you going to call 'rat' Mum? It is right here! Hurry!"

"Rat!"

The judge said, "Yes."

Then onto the hay bales and through the tunnel. All in 42 seconds.

I was so proud of Rio. I have read about how many dog breeds' sense of smell is amazing and much stronger than ours, and about search and rescue dogs, contraband dogs, and others with similar talents. But I never before saw a dog's nose in action in person, and not with my very own dog. This really blew me away. We decided to continue with this sport. Rio seemed to greatly enjoy himself.

Showtime! We signed up for a Barn Hunt Association Instinct Test, in Robbinsville, New Jersey. Rio found the rat in just seconds, I called it, and he passed the test!

Thus we moved to the next level, Novice. We competed at a few trials in East Stroudsburg, Pennsylvania. The first time we scored an NQ, my fault. I was too anxious and did not read Rio accurately, so called the rat too early. As the location of the rat is moved around the ring every few competitors, it is easy for a dog's sensitive nose to detect where a rat had been just minutes before, and signal that is where it still is. But I did not give up. I needed to work harder and understand when Rio was actually finding a live rat and how he marked it.

Rio's most amazing run occurred the second run of that day. I was waiting in line outside with Rio for our turn to enter the large hall where the Barn Hunt was taking place. Behind me was a very happy lady with an Airedale, who explained to me that her dog is of the breed that was bred to locate rat nests on the banks of rivers. She was so proud that he won first place in the morning run. I thought about leaving right there and then, but decided to give it another try.

Seconds later we entered the ring and stood inside the start box area, marked by the four small cones. The judge instructed me to take Rio's lead and collar off him and go when ready. I had barely removed his collar when Rio bolted past the tunnel and bales of straw in front of us, heading to the opposite right corner, about 20 or so feet away. I ran after him and watched with anticipation. He stood tensely facing the bales of straw like a pointing dog would, so focused.

Suddenly, quite impatiently, Rio turned his head back and forth, looking at me then to the straw bale and saying frantically, "It's the rat! Call it Mum! Hurry up, please! It's the rat!"

So I did, the judge said, "Yes!" and I sent Rio through the tunnel and onto a bale of straw. He did all this in 27 seconds! I was amazed and delighted.

We qualified and waited outside for all the runs to be completed. We were thrilled to get our Q ribbon, then the judge called out the ribbon placements. She smiled and said, "In first place, with a run of twenty-seven seconds, is Rio!"

How proud I am of you dear Rio! My Belgian prince came in first, even over dogs bred for rat hunting.

"Wow. That is pretty cool," I thought.

Rio went on to earn his Novice title, then we took a break to get him more used to tunnels with 90-degree turns. As with curved agility tunnels, he does not like going into dark places. We would like to return to Barn Hunt training to work on tunnels and refresh his skills. Stay tuned!

CHAPTER 37

The Nose Knows

"Watching your dog do nose work, or any kind of scenting work your dog has instinct to do, is simply amazing."

—*Joni*

$\mathcal{N}$ose work is a relatively new and fun scenting sport, although the general idea of dogs tracking and detecting a certain scent, such as that of a missing person, bombs, drugs, agricultural products, diseased bees, and so on, is not new.

I read that dogs primarily communicate by using their sense of smell, and that is why a blind and deaf dog may still do just fine tracking a scent if allowed to use his instinctive scenting ability. Certain breeds of dogs have a stronger ability than others, an uncanny genius to track scent. For example, the Blood Hound is famous for the police tracking work it has done throughout history.

A dog's sense of smell is so important that the dog may rely on it to interpret its world, similar to how a human relies on sight. I have read that it has been estimated that the percent of a dogs brain that is focused on analyzing scents is about 40 times larger than that of a person, so no wonder dogs can identify scents much better than humans do. Their abilities may vary depending on the breed of dog, the ability of the specific dog, and type of material used in the search.

According to research, humans may have an estimated five million sensory cells in their nose, while certain dogs may have over 220 million. A fascinating book to read about dog scenting ability is *Scent and the Scenting Dog* by William G. Syrotuck.

Dogs rely on scent to tell them all about a person or another dog. Just by scent, they can tell if the other dog is a male or female, where they have been and what they ate, and if they are ready to mate. Recent research has also confirmed that via their sense of smell, dogs can tell a lot about a person, such as whether they have cancer, or if they are going to have a seizure.

There have been many studies performed to see if dogs can detect cancer. In research testing, dogs have been able to smell breath or urine samples of patients, or sniff near their cancerous body parts, even in early stages of the cancer, and identify breast, bladder, colorectal, lung, prostrate, and other cancers with high accuracy. Researchers believe that may be because they can smell volatile organic compounds of certain types.

Certain dogs' sense of smell is so acute that they can smell multiple scents at one time and differentiate between them. For example, while humans can smell one type of scent, such as a cooking sauce, many dogs are able to identify each individual ingredient in that sauce.

Many dogs have a keen sense of perception as well as smell, and can learn to identify signs from their owners that something is not right. Similarly, some dogs learn to tell when someone is becoming anxious and needs medicine, and others can learn to alert type one diabetic humans that their blood sugar is off before the person tests her/his blood. Dogs have also alerted their owners that a heart attack was about to occur, or that their blood pressure has changed significantly.

As such, it is not a surprise that many dogs can easily be trained to locate certain scents for competitive sport purposes, such as birch, anise and clove, as used in the National Association of Canine Scent Work (NACSW) odor recognition tests and trials.

Handlers take nose work classes to learn how to work with their dog to identify the various scents, and usually the birch scent is taught first. Many dogs can find the scent easily with some basic training. Sometimes, what is more difficult is for the handler to learn to quickly and accurately identify when their dog has found the scent.

The dog may be taught to signal in a certain way that they have found the scent, perhaps by sniffing around the edges of the box in which the scent is hidden, keeping its nose on the box, sitting by or staring at the box, or by pointing at or pawing the box.

For NACSW, the first nose work test is the birch odor recognition test (ORT), where 12 boxes are lined up on the floor, in two columns of six. One of the boxes contains the "source," which is usually a few Q-tips containing the birch scent. This "hot" box is mixed in with the other boxes and left to set for about one-half hour or more before the ORT so the scent can settle.

The dog and handler enter the room and are given three minutes to locate the scent. If the dog finds the scent and the handler believes the dog is correct, the handler will call out, "Alert!" A similar odor recognition test is available for the clove and anise scents.

Once each ORT is passed, the door is open for various levels of titles with NACSW, including those done in indoor, outdoor, and car searches. It is a fun sport where dogs can enjoy using their scenting ability. The United Kennel Club is another great venue for nose work. Myrrh and vetiver scents are used by the United Kennel Club in addition to birch, anise and clove.

After many lessons, I tried the birch ORT with both Rio and Romeo. Though very successful with searches in class, I NQ'd with both dogs at the ORT. Both dogs did great during training, but in the ORT they were different dogs.

Rio entered the room and started his sniffing, probably knowing exactly where the birch was, but having too good a time smelling all the scents on the ground left by the other dogs. Because many of the places where the ORTs are held are dog training schools, there are plenty of scents around.

Romeo, on the other hand, is a star at finding birch at home and in training class, but when we entered the ORT test in a location he had never before been, he became insecure from being in a new place, got frazzled, and ran to the door.

I know that, bottom line, I need to improve my training of Rio and Romeo. They are both very smart and capable of doing this so well at home and in training class. Both are also very different in how they search and have different training needs, and I need to continue to work to best help them to succeed. This training must continue to include practice at new places, so that when we go to an ORT at a place they have never been, they will not be as distracted as they are now.

Although we are not ready for competition, we still do training, and I find that setting up some hides at home at least once a week is great fun and good practice for them. They love trying to pick out which box the birch is in, or where multiple hides are hidden in various rooms.

I also take them to different parks and other places to introduce them to new areas and build their confidence. Nose work is a wonderful sport that many attest is good for dogs with issues.

∞

Tracking is another exciting scenting sport Rio, Romeo and I have dabbled in over the last few years. We took a two-day seminar on the basics of tracking, and some lessons a couple of years ago with Lisa (one of our favorite instructors), and hope to return to tracking again soon. It is a wonderful sport where dogs use their natural nose-scenting ability to find the scent of humans, or articles dropped by a human. In real life, dogs are trained for search and rescue of humans, whether missing persons or criminals, and even other dogs or other animals, as we were to find out with Romeo.

For competition, dogs are trained to follow the trail of a track-setting person to find an object, usually a glove or a sock that has been placed at the end of the track by that person. The tracks are of various levels of difficulty. The dogs work with their handler as a team, but do not get assistance from their handlers. The handler has to rely on the dog to do its job, which is sometimes very difficult to do. In American Kennel Club competition, it is a pass/fail test. And unlike some other sports, only one qualifying score earns that level's title.

The American Kennel Club offers the Tracking Dog title (TD), Tracking Dog Urban title (TDU), Tracking Dog Excellent title (TDX), Variable Surface Tracking title (VST) and Champion Tracker (CT). Each title offers different challenges, such as longer tracks, more directional changes, sometimes challenging the dog to locate a scent that crosses around a building, across a road, or in an urban environment. It is a fascinating sport that we hope to continue sometime in the future.

CHAPTER 38

Agility

"Climb to new heights, venture into the dark
and through unknown paths, do not be afraid,
I will guide you."

—*Joni*

"I'm afraid of heights and the dark, Mum!" Rio told me when we started taking agility lessons. I have always enjoyed watching dogs doing agility. Agility is a sport in which the competitor handler/dog team must complete within a certain time a challenging course of obstacles, which vary depending on the venue but may include tunnels, various types of jumps — including bar jumps and tire jumps, contact equipment such as the A-Frame, dog walk, teeter-totter (also known as the see-saw), weave poles, barrels and hoops. Time and accuracy are very important.

There are various venues for competition in the United States, including the American Kennel Club, United

Kennel Club and the North American Dog Agility Council (NADAC), among others.

I thought I had a good plan for Rio's success. We would train, practice, and practice and train some more, then we would enter some trials. But as I've heard, "people plan, and God laughs!"

We went to lots of training. We have taken lessons from some of the best in the field in our area, at St. Hubert's, Kellar's, Mary Lou's training classes, and Vince with his agility confidence course, locally, and not so locally. And I thank each and every one of my instructors for their patience and creativity in training and motivation.

But it gets more complicated. I always hoped Rio could earn a title in agility, but it has not been that easy for us. Rio is a show dog, but has his issues. Rio is afraid of heights, so we have issues with the dog walk. He is good at the lower-level dog walk but not at full competition height. And sometimes, Rio decides he does not want to go into a tunnel, because it is too dark and there may be a bogeyman inside!

But after lots and lots of practice, Rio earned a Dog Scouts of America Obstacle Course I badge. This involved Rio doing an A-Frame at five-foot height, doing a straight fully-extended open tunnel on cue, and jumping a variety of jumps, such as winged and bar jumps. Also, we had to submit a video of Rio taking an A-Frame, open tunnel, and jumping in succession off-lead, working parallel or ahead of me, the handler. I am so proud he could do this, and thank our instructor Mary Lou for her patience and fine training!

Because of Rio's fear of heights and the dark making him not so happy with the dog walk and tunnels, I thought I would focus on jumps. He is awesome at jumps, so I trialed him in a NADAC competition at an outside field at St. Hubert's. To my surprise and the evident surprise of the judge, he did all the jumps, but in between each jump, he dropped his head and sniffed the entire time when on the ground between jumps! Rio apologized to me, saying, "I am so sorry Mum! So many scents there, Mum, and so little time!" Despite days like that, with a lot of praise and encouragement we have made some progress.

To address Rio's fear of curved tunnels, we tried many things and very positive training. Rio will finally do a tunnel, most times, on command. Our dear instructor, Niki, tried everything to get Rio through the curved tunnel. He finally consistently ran through at top speed when she asked a student with a young bitch to stand the bitch at the opposite end of the tunnel. Good strategy, it worked and Rio ran through the tunnel at record speed — but unfortunately, this does not work in a competition when I cannot have one of Rio's girlfriends on the other end of the tunnel. But at least Rio is no longer afraid of the bogeymen in the tunnels and does them most of the time! Thank you, Niki!

As far as the other equipment, Rio is great with hoops and going around barrels as used in the NADAC venue. A-Frames usually are his friend and we have got the weave poles down pretty well; though Rio is not fast, he is now focused and likes them pretty much.

We will continue to practice and hopefully go further. I purchased some of our own agility jumps, tunnels, hoops and weave poles. But like me (and maybe he gets this from me), Rio is still afraid of heights, so the dog walk at full height and the teeter-totter are our last big challenges.

For Romeo, agility is one of his favorite activities. He earned his American Kennel Club Agility Course Tests 1 and 2 (ACT 1 and ACT 2), entry-level events from the American Kennel Club. Romeo has used this sport as a release for his fears. When he is in a class, he is nervous. But show Romeo a tunnel, and he is through it. Show him a dog walk, and onto it he goes. Show him an A-Frame and he is over it.

I started showing him in the NADAC venue and will continue again. It is I who has held Romeo back from more agility training, having sprained my ankle in agility class. We have not competed recently, but we continue to do training in our yard and I do plan to start up again soon.

Along the way, we were told that excellent online training classes for agility are Susan Garrett's Handling 360 and Agility Nation. She offers training seminars and videos about every aspect of training a dog for agility competition. Her instruction came highly recommended to me by a very nice gentleman at one of the Belgian Tervuren National agility competitions.

Susan's courses are fun and are very good positive training for your dog. We look forward to her training, and soon, I am hoping to buy a dog walk and teeter so we can work on Rio's fears. We are still trying, and my goal is to do so until we succeed!

CHAPTER 39

Trick or Treat and Other Fun Sports

"Come with me, trust me, let's venture out, do new
things together, explore, and grow."

—*Joni*

*T*raining a dog to perform tricks is nothing new.
People have probably trained dogs to do tricks
since dogs started interacting with humans so
long ago. However, dog titling for trick performance is
a relatively new activity here in the United States.

Several years ago, we discovered a new dog training website, *Do More With Your Dog*, started by Kyra
Sundance. It is an organization that encourages people
to train their dogs with positive training and to do fun
tricks with them. Tricks are a lot of fun and can be used
in many venues in addition to just having a fun time with
your dog. I love to teach my boys tricks, and it is fun
having Rio do the tricks for people at the nursing home
and hospice and making them smile.

Do More With Your Dog offers trick titles at various increasingly difficult levels. We started trick training at home and Rio earned his first trick title, Novice Trick Dog, followed by his Intermediate, Advanced and Expert Trick Dog titles.

A couple of years ago, the American Kennel Club started offering trick dog titles and also began recognizing titles from the *Do More With Your Dog* organization, up to the level of Advanced as of a certain date. Thus both Rio and Romeo earned Trick Dog Advanced titles with the American Kennel Club.

The American Kennel Club also announced their new top trick dog title Trick Dog Performer, which requires that each dog perform 10 tricks from a trick list on the American Kennel Club website and submit a video of the dogs performing those tricks. This was so much fun because I taught Rio and Romeo some new tricks.

One of my favorites was teaching them to play a child's piano-like sound toy. On command, I taught each dog to lift his paw and press the large keyboard buttons. Each button, when pressed, makes a noise such as a cat meowing. It was such fun for all of us, and they so enjoyed the noises the toy made when they interacted with it.

I asked Lisa (also a trick instructor, in addition to nose work, tracking and other sports) if she would video our performance, and she was glad to help. I submitted the videos to the American Kennel Club, along with a write-up for both Rio and Romeo, to give the American Kennel Club Evaluator an idea of what both dogs are like. I thanked them for offering more opportunities for titles, as these titles are a permanent tribute to both dogs and our wonderful relationships. I was thrilled that Rio and Romeo both earned the American Kennel Club Trick Dog Performer title!

I recently discovered that you can earn trick titles remotely by video, through another organization, Cyber

K9, and look forward to starting work on some new trick titles with them. We are also very happy that *Do More With Your Dog* now offers a new program called Stunt Dog. Stunt Dog titles are earned by a demonstration of showmanship and tricks in live ring trials, performed before a live audience, and are also recognized by the American Kennel Club.

So as with other sports, I read the rules, we practiced and practiced, and I entered the first ring trial held in our area for Stunt Dog titles. I am very proud that Rio earned his Novice and Open Stunt Dog titles on our first try!

∞

On our training journey, we learned about the dog sport Parkour, and discovered the International Dog Parkour Association and All Dogs Parkour online. These groups encourage people to get outside and do Parkour activities with their dogs, in some ways similar to human Parkour.

For Parkour, handlers train their dogs to do things like jumping, climbing, crawling under obstacles, climbing into containers, putting two front paws or all four paws on objects, balancing on objects, climbing onto moving obstacles, and so on, with encouragement to do these things in new places outside.

Parkour helps both handler and dog with learning, teamwork, and building confidence as a team and as an individual. It can be a lot of fun and challenging, perhaps adventurous at times. It is very rewarding, being a non-competitive sport in that you 'compete' with yourself and can earn titles for your dog after completing certain requirements in each title category. Most importantly, it must be done safely.

I tried Parkour with Rio and Romeo, and both earned their Parkour Dog in Training title (PKD-T) and Novice title (PKD-N) with the International Dog Parkour Association.

We then tried parkour with All Dogs Parkour and just cannot stop doing Parkour! They are a wonderful, fun Internet group, and we are working on earning titles with them for both Rio and Romeo. It is a challenging group with seemingly unlimited opportunities, and both boys love doing Parkour. It is such fun for all of us! Stay tuned!

We have discovered new parks and other places in our township and nearby towns in search of places to do Parkour, and have greatly expanded our horizons. Simple things the boys know how to do, such as jumping over an agility or obedience/rally jump or going around a barrel, is expanded upon with Parkour as we now go to the park and they are called upon to jump over a fallen log or branch, crawl under a park bench or fence bar, and go around a lamp post or between two trees.

Rio and Romeo are much more conscious of and confident in their surroundings and abilities, and at times I can see them analyzing a situation to see if they can perhaps jump over something or if it is better to go under it or around it. Practicing Parkour has given both dogs much more confidence in our neighborhood and park walks, exhibited by the confidence they have in going off trail, jumping over logs or small streams without showing concern.

Just recently, after a nor'easter snow storm, Rio climbed onto tall snow drifts, sank into the snow and jumped back out, and did this all very confidently, something he would not do last year.

It has been a very educational and worthwhile experience for them and me. Not only do they have more confidence in what they do, I have more confidence in them, their judgment, and their safety.

There are so many other dog sports, many targeted specifically towards certain breeds, such as field trials for hunting dogs and trials for herding dogs like Rio. And there are many sports that do not always depend on the type of breed, but rather on what the specific dog can do, such as lure-coursing. I know many Belgian owners who have earned top lure coursing titles with their dogs who love the sport. When I tried Rio and Romeo with lure coursing, both at separate times, each had the same reaction. They ran after the bag that was attached to the conveyor string being pulled in a circle.

Once they reached the bag, they sniffed it, realized what it was, and stopped chasing it. They both looked at me as if to say, "Mum, this is only a plastic bag. Why would I want to chase this around and around? How boring." Then they moved on to sniffing more interesting scents. Needless to say we did not pursue lure coursing.

Dock diving is another fun sport for dogs who love the water. Dogs compete in trials where they run and jump from a dock into the air, trying to catch a toy or bumper device, and land safely in a deep swimming pool. They compete to see how far a dog can jump off a dock into the pool, while successfully catching the item.

Our first two dogs, Shaolin and Marly, loved water and swimming in our swimming pool. Shaolin would dive off the side of our in-ground pool just to go after the Frisbee we had thrown (upside down so it would float) at the far end of the pool. He and Marly (who gracefully went down the pool stairs) both raced for that Frisbee. Sometimes they swam back side by side, each with a side of the Frisbee in their mouths. So fun to watch!

I did not know about all these dog sports back then when Shaolin and Marly were with us. I would bet that both of them would have loved dock diving.

CHAPTER 40

Shall We Dance?

*"Dance with me my friend, let's dance and enjoy today
and every day, as if there are no more tomorrows."*

—*Joni*

I love to sing and dance. My dad had a band when he was young, playing saxophone, clarinet, and piano, and often played records at home (33s and other old recordings) of Strauss waltzes, polkas, and a variety of World War II big band and other music by Benny Goodman, Glenn Miller, Louis Armstrong, Billie Holiday, Frank Sinatra and Johnny Mathis.

Dad also played piano alongside my brother, William, who is also a very talented pianist. Mom could be heard daily singing love songs, while Pat loved to sing Marilyn Monroe and Marlene Dietrich songs, and new Broadway musical songs, especially those sung by Liza Minelli. She loved Liza's mom, Judy Garland, and her songs and movies, especially her performance of *Over the Rainbow* from *The Wizard of Oz*.

SHALL WE DANCE?

I grew up with music as part of my day and it became a part of me. Thus, when I was young, it was natural that I loved to sing and dance. I loved all kinds of music.

When I met Joe, we started taking ballroom dancing lessons. I had always wanted a dance partner since the days when Dad played music at home. Joe and I enjoyed the samba, tango, rumba, and other Latin dances, and loved dancing so much that we traveled hours to find a ballroom with ballroom dancing and music.

Guess what? After we moved in together, he did not want to dance anymore. I would have to get him to a wedding and coax him to have a glass of wine to loosen up, then he might dance a dance or two with me.

At home, for years while Joe traveled, I would often put on my favorite CDs and dance by myself. I had fun and it was great exercise.

And then … Rio entered the scene. I finally had a new dance partner!

I had seen dog-dancing videos on the Internet. Some of my instructors referred me to specific YouTube videos, where you'll find some of the best dancing performances by searching for dog or canine dancing and Crufts, an international dog show held annually in the United Kingdom.

Shortly after watching videos of some of the best dancers at Crufts, I searched for a local dog-dancing organization and discovered the World Canine Freestyle Organization (WCFO). I became a member and discovered dog-dancing can be a lot of fun. You dance to music of your own choice with your best furry friend.

It is exciting to select favorite music you think you and your dog can dance to, then choreograph your dance, and practice, practice, practice. You can even costume up with your dog and compete in person! Alternatively, because sometimes it is quite far to travel, you can join a group like WCFO which offers titles by mail or online.

The sport is great fun. You work with your canine partner as a team to master both simple and complex dance techniques. Best of all for me, I found out that Rio thinks it is so much fun dancing with me!

After reading the WCFO website and becoming familiar with their rules, I decided we would try to earn the entry-level Bronze Bar Musical Freestyle title. Freestyle is choreographed dancing of handlers and their dogs to music. We filled out the application for the test and mailed it in, and soon received the packet which outlined what we must do.

The requirements for the Bronze Bar included spins, leg weaves, and heeling in two large circles, one to the left, one to the right, and a backup. This was all to be done to music which we could select. I love all kinds of music, so I had great fun selecting a song, though this was not an easy task. I listened to many dozens of CDs, and while on my way to work I would listen to songs on the radio, too.

The winning song, the song that seemed to say what I felt towards Rio, was *Time of My Life*, from the movie *Dirty Dancing*. I chose that song because it truly is what I have been having with Rio — the time of my life.

Rio has lit up my life like a fireworks celebration. I was stuck in a very dark place, and he not only helped me move forward, but we climbed many challenging mountains together and reached new heights. And had enormous fun doing it!

He brings many smiles to my face every day with his humor and charm, and always wants to keep me on the go. Rio has kept me busy, and enticed me to join in and try things I never would have thought of, making new friends along the way, giving me joy and returning my confidence and zest for life — and I owe it all to him.

I printed out the words to the song. The time for our dance was limited to one minute, 30 seconds, plus or minus 15 seconds.

As our next step, we took a class at Kellar's Canine Academy with Renee, who teaches dance classes and is a star with her dogs in many dog sports, including rally and herding. She helped get us started in doggie dancing, giving us ideas on how to select music, types of moves we can consider, as well as our timing. Thank you, Renee!

I enjoyed choreographing our moves to the music, and we practiced often. Finally, I thought we were ready. I asked our instructor, Lisa, if she would video us doing our dance in one of our classes. She was very happy to do so.

We went outside to the horse track area behind her training barn with her boom box and my CD, and off Rio and I went into our dance. I thought we both did a nice job together! I submitted the video and was overjoyed that Rio earned his first dance title! I was so thrilled that I framed the certificate and hung it on one of Rio's title walls at home. I love the WCFO and hope to continue to participate in their dancing contests and events.

I was very happy when WCFO announced they were to participate in a new event near us — the first event of its type — as part of the dog exposition at the Meadowlands in Secaucus. We entered the event for exhibition purposes only, knowing we were not ready to compete, and choreographed a skit of sorts.

Again, I listened to dozens of songs, this time selecting the music *With You On My Arm* from *La Cage aux Folles*. It is a fun song, with two people taking turns singing. One says that he cannot dance, and the other insists that he can. I thought it would be a perfect dance or skit for Rio, who can dance, but at times is not so motivated to do so.

We had the dance routine down pretty well and I could not wait to do it at the show. However, at the show, Rio was a bit overwhelmed by all the excitement and the noise.

"Mum, I am really embarrassed to be dancing in front of all these people! I would rather be sniffing all these good scents on the floor from other dogs," he told me.

He danced some, sniffed some, danced, sniffed ... oh, my dear sniffer! My funny little boy thought this was a sniff-festival and was having a fun time sniffing while hundreds of people watched!

I laughed. I am learning to laugh at myself and what we do sometimes, and to not be self-conscious anymore. Perhaps that comes with age, but in any event, we love dancing, so we will keep on with it and try for another title or two.

We recently discovered another online dance venue, *Poised for Success Freestyle*. It is an educational group that offers titles at various levels of skill. The skills from the beginning levels set the groundwork and ready your dance team for the freestyle dancing skills required in the higher titling levels. The skill sets required are fun to learn and have resulted in great team-building for me and Rio. Their website even offers video examples of the dancing skills required for the titles. Rio just earned his first title at the Overture Division and we are working now on the Melody Division. I am very excited.

As Rio matures, I hope to continue dancing with him, as it is a sport we can do as we age together. It was heart-warming to see a team competing at the Meadowlands competition who danced beautifully with very nice team-work. At the end of the performance, the young lady announced, with tears streaming down her face, that her dog has had cancer for quite some time, but the dancing motivates him to go on because he just loves dancing with her so much. I hope Rio and I can dance together at a ripe old age.

Later that summer, our dancing continued. One evening, I had an unexpected, very enchanting surprise. Rio asked me to dance with him. No kidding. Really.

It was a warm night in the mid-80s, and humid. The air was scented with sweet-smelling honeysuckle and roses and was absolutely beautiful. I had cut the lawn in the back and Rio did not look happy that I was doing that and not giving him any attention. When done, I fed Rio and Romeo, then sat on the swing in our backyard to relax before making dinner.

I was tired after working all day, driving some three hours, then cutting the grass, and doing about 17,000 steps on my pedometer for the day. After eating, Rio walked over to me and stared at me, smiling, with a mischievous look on his face. He is so smart and cute, I could not ignore him. He was up to something.

I have found that the more I communicate with Rio, the better our relationship is. Just like a human, if I ignore him, he gets frustrated, lies down and shows he is bored. He loves mental stimulation and physical activity and loves to interact with me a lot.

When Rio stood there staring at me, I was very curious as to what he wanted.

"What do you want, sweetie?" I asked.

Playful and full of energy, Rio took a step backwards, still staring at me, encouraging me to go with him. I stood up and he backed up some more, still staring into my eyes.

I was puzzled for a moment, but then a light bulb went on.

"Rio, do you want to dance with me?" He looked intrigued, grinned, and kept staring, his tail wagging slowly.

"Mum, may I have this dance please? Would you dance with me this beautiful summer eve, Mum?" Rio pleaded.

"Yes, my dear Rio, I would love to."

I started singing *Time of My Life*, we had practiced it for so long for the WCFO title.

"I've had the time of my life and I owe it all to you ...."

I held out my hand and he gave me his paw and kissed me. He backed up and I followed, then I backed up and he followed, then a Schutzhund turn... "someone to stand by me."

Three spins together. Then more backups, a hand touch, and then he danced through my legs in a figure eight move. And our dance went on....

Yes, Rio wanted to dance with me that day and have some special interaction with me. I really believe he did. He was so happy after we danced, and we cheered for him. My little dance partner, my buddy, Rio.

The next evening, Rio was in the mood again. He asked me to dance. And so we danced, joyfully, in our own little world. We had a marvelous time! Joe was witness to Rio's dance proposals both days. And as time goes by, Rio now frequently asks me to dance in the early morning before I go to work, so we do so for a minute or two, both of us happy and excited to be with each other.

I do believe there is a little person or elf within Rio. I know it may sound crazy, but he is so in tune with me and my thoughts and emotions, and we communicate very well. I have never experienced this before with any person or animal.

Rio is a very special dog and dancer. And to top it off, Rio has two left feet, and is still a much better dancer than I!

CHAPTER 41

General Training

*"Love me, hug me, make me happy, walk with me,
dance with me, make me feel safe, and I will do
anything for you."*

—*Joni*

*I*t has taken a long time, but I have learned to improvise and use alternative rewards while training Rio and Romeo. I always use positive training, and instead of being able to rely consistently on food (and never on toys) as a positive reinforcement, I use a mix of training motivators.

I learned over several years that for Rio, it is all about me being positive and happy. I must be that way to try to always keep Rio playful and joyful, in order to motivate him to want to give me the behaviors I request.

First and foremost, I use myself as Rio's motivator, with energy and enthusiasm that I show in my expressions, movements, along with the key words, smiles, hugs, and praise that I use to reinforce correct behavior.

At a trial, which nowadays is mainly rally, I tell him before we enter the ring, "It is Showtime!" and he knows he is going to perform. I scratch or pet him and get him excited about going into the ring.

When he performs well in the ring, or has a great training class, I praise him and clap and smile cheek to cheek. I often give him a quick body rub, scratch, or pats to reward him. These are what most consistently motivate Rio. When he knows he has done what I have asked of him, he is very proud.

A big help to me has been Karen Pryor's clicker training, and we practice it often in class and at home. It is positive reinforcement training, and Rio responds very well to it. When I mark his correct behavior with a clicker or a positive word, I can see the joy on Rio's face. He knows he has performed what I have asked. I can see a lightbulb go on when he realizes he has understood me. When he is in a food-driven mood, I use food, otherwise I use praise in conjunction with the clicker. When a clicker is not available, I use a word such as, "Yes!" or, "Yay!" along with lots of happy pats and scratches so Rio knows he did well and is happy and excited.

For those times that Rio is in the mood for them, I am always ready with some very attractive treats in my pocket. Those times are rare, but I make a lot of progress when they happen.

In addition to my behavior, I have also used other dogs and dog scents as motivators, though both of these have been more difficult to train. Being very social, he loves being with other dogs in a training or show ring. Though it has taken a while to train, Rio has learned that if he performs well at a rally trial, he will likely have the opportunity to play or flirt with his girlfriends or other dogs afterwards — but he must perform in the ring first. Rio is always very excited about sniffing dog scents outside the show ring, thus often times I use the command, "Go sniff," after he performs well, as a reward as he leaves the show ring.

Training with Rio is fun, but Rio's learning span is short. I need to get to the point with the training quickly and do an activity a limited amount of times. Unlike Shaolin, who as a black Labrador would do a sit over and over again, dozens of times with the same enthusiasm, Rio gets bored quickly and may only do a few sits before he gets bored. He is a different kind of learner, so I must pace our training and do things strategically.

This strategy has worked well with my limited training time availability. I usually have only a few minutes in the morning and evening to do training on work days, so this still proves to be very productive for Rio, as well as Romeo, who are both quick learners.

We have also found many excellent Internet dog training resources that are wonderful because they offer new and innovative ways of thinking about training and help you learn what is best for your dog. Often, I just cannot find time on a regular basis to attend an in-person lesson, but the online courses can be done at my convenience, day or night, with very highly qualified instructors available from around the country. They are a fabulous asset.

We greatly enjoy the Denise Fenzi training classes found at the Fenzi Dog Sports Academy online, which offers a wide variety of training opportunities. The classes include behavioral, relationship-building, agility, nose-work, rally and freestyle, obedience, and other subjects, for both beginners and experts alike.

One of my favorite Fenzi courses is Imitation and Mimicry. The instructor teaches you how to teach your dog to watch you and imitate what you have just done. Once Rio and I got the gist of this, he has been able to mimic many of my actions very quickly. I love this course! Over time, I have taught Rio a small variety of tricks, and I ask him to do them and some mimicry for the residents in the nursing home as part of his visits. People enjoy watching him do tricks and are amazed by them, especially when we do mimicry.

I am still amazed by how Rio mimics my actions with minimal training. I have told Rio, "Do this," and then I spin around in a complete circle. I watch him focus on me, then suddenly, his mouth closes and he gets his "thinking cap" on. Then he proceeds to do a full spin in front of me.

I also taught Rio to imitate me when I lean over and put my right arm out to touch the ground in front of him, and then my left arm. Then he does the same with his front feet. He has also learned to sit when I tell him to, "do this," and I sit down onto a chair. It is a fun learning process for both of us and brings lots of smiles to people.

I have found so many accomplished trainers through the years and appreciate everything each and every one has done to help us along our journey of training experiences. We have taken many group and private classes in conformation, rally, obedience, nose work, agility, herding, dance, and other sports.

Some trainers are specific to one sport such as sheep herding, and others teach various sports. In some cases, we have brought to the attention of our instructors new dog sport opportunities that I discovered on the Internet, and they have graciously and patiently helped us with activities such as dog tricks, Parkour, and dog dancing. Some trainers we still train with, and I apologize to others because I have so little time and not enough financial resources to do everything. But it does not mean we will not be back to you at some point on another day.

Thank you, dear trainers, and to all, Happy Training!

CHAPTER 42

Visiting Angels With Fur

*"What is the essence of life? To serve others and
to do good."*

—Aristotle

I noticed that the American Kennel Club offered
Therapy Dog titles, and Dog Scouts offered Therapy
Dog badges to promote this precious community
involvement. I thought maybe this was our next journey
together.

Remembering how Rio did so well when I took him
to visit Mom in the nursing home, and knowing he had
matured and was very obedient with a good disposition,
I believed we could do this. It was time for us to become
certified as a therapy dog team.

I heard that Kellar's Canine Academy held Pet Partners
therapy dog team tests, so looked up the Pet Partner organization on the Internet. Pet Partners has been a therapy
animal organization since the 1970s, not only for dogs,
but for many animals. Their website says, "Touching

lives and improving health through the power of therapy animals." I thought that was marvelous and really wanted to help people with sweet Rio, so decided to take the plunge and get certified.

Pet Partners has a number of requirements. I had to read a lot of educational materials about Pet Partners and therapy dog work, then take an online test. Rio and I were also required to take an in-person team test, simulating a nursing home visit. We practiced our obedience and I tried to familiarize him with various items he might encounter in a hospital or nursing home environment such as crutches, wheelchairs, and walkers.

The test involved role-playing, just as if we were in a nursing home or hospital. Test criteria included: accepting a friendly stranger, accepting petting, heeling on loose lead, walking through a crowd, reactions to distractions, sitting on cue, down on cue, stays and coming when called, reaction to other dogs, reaction to clumsy petting and a restraining hug, reaction to a staggering or yelling person, how the dog reacts to angry yelling and being bumped from behind, complying with the command, "leave it," and what the dog does when offered a treat. The dog may be rated as Level 2 (highest/good ranking, able to visit Complex Environments), Level 1 (visits limited to Predictable Environments), Not Ready (NR) or Not Appropriate (NA). If the dog and owner pass the test, the team receives a determination of being qualified to visit in Predictable Environments or Complex Environments.

We passed our first in-person Pet Partners test, with Rio qualifying to visit in Predictable Environments. At the time, however, we were not able to take on an assignment because of other commitments. We retested as a therapy dog team a couple of years later and passed again, this time ready to find a local nursing home that would like us to start visits. Rio qualified for Complex

Environments, which means we could visit residents in all types of environments.

I checked the Pet Partners website for available assignments and was thrilled there was a facility just nine miles from us that was looking for a therapy dog team to come visit. A new nursing home, rehabilitation center and hospice facility had just opened. I contacted them, and their Activities Director, Carrie, invited us in for an interview.

It was a wonderful time to start on our assignment, with both the facility and us as a team beginning our work. The nursing home was so new that our first visit was to only one resident. The facility quickly filled, and all three floors are now occupied. We became busier with each visit, visiting everyone who wanted a visit from a therapy dog. Then we also began volunteering at a separate hospice facility.

We love our therapy dog team visits. Out of all the activities we have taken on, this has been the most rewarding for us. The residents greatly enjoy our visits, though all the credit goes to Rio. They are always so happy to see him, and he always brightens their day.

It is well known that interaction with dogs, and other animals, can improve human health and well-being. Dogs bring a sense of comfort and serenity that only unconditional love can bring. They have a way of bringing joy, love, and happiness to people.

Dogs can elevate one's mood and have a calming effect, reduce anxiety or depression, and may even diminish physical pain. Often a visit from a therapy dog can increase socialization and decrease feelings of isolation in a person. A simple visit from a dog can bring a smile to someone's face and make them forget about their pain or troubles for a few minutes.

I believe with my heart and soul that Rio helps to do this. Rio brings much joy to the residents we visit, many of them people who once had dogs and/or other pets and no longer can have them for age, health, or other reasons. Many have thanked us from their hearts for visiting them and making their day.

It is a blessing to see the positive change in a resident who a moment ago did not want to see Rio because of anxiety or pain — but then melts into a smile when Rio nudges or kisses them. Several residents who have lost their vision have been overjoyed just to pet and hug Rio, and many people who never had a dog, or were once afraid of dogs, are very happy to see and pet Rio once they experience his consistently sweet personality and demeanor.

To the lucky ones on each visit whom Rio gives a kiss to (he sometimes is a little stingy with his kisses), they feel like they have won the lottery. Indeed, Rio does magic at the nursing home and hospice. He is truly an angel with fur.

Many residents want to know all about Rio, how old he was when I got him, what he is like at home, what he likes to do, and our dog show experiences. When people meet Rio for the first time, I introduce him, "Rio says, 'hello,' and he is so happy to meet you." I tell them his name is Rio, but that he would like me to point out that he has a few other names, mainly "good boy," and "I love you."

I kid you not. Rio does think his name is "I love you." I have let Rio out in the backyard, then after a while, opened the door to call him back inside and yelled, "I love you!" What a surprise — he ran right to me!

In addition to talking about Rio, people enjoy talking about their pets at home, pets they once had, their families, fun days of traveling, and of happier days. They share with us their favorite memories, stories both happy and sad, and their personal achievements and talents. Sometimes they share their dreams and their fears, and sometimes I am lucky to meet their families, who are so happy to finally meet Rio.

Our visits have become so important to many people. We visit regularly because people look forward to our visits. We try to make each visit a special one, and for the holidays, I always try to be festive and have a holiday leash for Rio and holiday necklaces or sweaters for me. Being a volunteer is such an honor, a very heartwarming assignment I am very proud to do with Rio.

We have had so much fun and many memorable times. One day, we walked down the hall and one lady's face lit up when she saw Rio. She could not wait to see him and find out more about him. Rio knew she was new to the nursing home, and walked up to her to welcome her. She petted and scratched him, then happily talked about her prior pets and smiled as she thanked us so much for visiting her.

Afterward, the activities assistant told us she was thrilled by the lady's reaction to Rio. The lady had arrived a few days ago and had not been very sociable or outgoing until she met Rio. This was a big breakthrough for her and the start of good things.

Another resident was bedridden. When we arrived at her room, the lights were off and the blinds closed, making the room very gray. The activities assistant asked if she would like to see Rio.

"Yes, I would love to," she replied very softly.

Without direction from me, Rio walked right over to her outstretched arm and kissed her palm. He looked into her eyes so gently, ever caring with his loving, almond-shaped eyes.

A huge smile lit up her face. She weakly stroked his soft coat over and over, speaking softly to Rio. I had tears in my eyes when she said, "Rio, you are my best friend." His visit meant so much to her.

Another day, a very jovial gentleman, Mr. J., was having fun flirting with one of his lady friends. She joked with him, but it was clear he was not making any progress with her. Instead, she gave Rio her full attention, sweetly talking with Rio and scratching and petting him. To our surprise, Mr. J. suddenly asked her, "If I looked like Rio, would you love me then?" He then laughed, and we all joined in celebrating Rio. Another day, all in good fun, Mr. J. asked one of the activities assistants, "If I walked on four feet like Rio, would you love me, too?"

Mr. J. loves to see Rio every time we visit. Before we leave, he always blesses Rio and thanks us so much for coming in to see everyone.

Recently, Rio stopped by to see Ms. J., a big fan of his. Ms. J. is elderly and quite frail, sitting in her wheelchair. She became very excited when she saw Rio and reached out to pet him.

"Rio is a very special boy, isn't he?" she whispered.

"Yes, he is," I nodded.

She then said, "You love him very much, do you not?" and reached out to hold my hand. "You are very special too, and your love for him is more than that, isn't it?" she asked.

"Yes," I smiled, as tears welled up in my eyes. Yes, Rio is so very special. I love him so much, it breaks my heart.

In addition to bringing joy to the residents, Rio has uplifted many family members and friends of the nursing home and hospice residents. Often times, hospice provides the last care for people, thus we have been blessed many times to help family members through a very tough time just after the passing of their loved one.

Where only a few moments before people have not been approachable, we have had occasions where in the break room, they see Rio and rush to him for a hug. They came for some water or a snack after a very difficult and exhausting day, only to see Rio's angelic and understanding face and wagging tail offering them love. We are so glad to be there for them and help in whatever way we can to make their days a bit easier. Dogs are truly angels with fur.

In addition to assisting the residents and their families, it has been very important to many of the staff to experience regular Rio visits. Every day for them can be very busy and stressful, and at times tragic. It has been heartwarming on so many of our visits when staff have rushed down the hall or out of their office to give a hug to Rio, sometimes saying, "I need a therapy dog today too." Rio greets them joyfully.

To enhance our visits with the residents and make them smile, I have worked on special dog tricks and some doggie dance moves with Rio. All of these bring smiles and joy not only to the residents, but to the staff who find a joyful moment in their day when Rio comes to visit. Every visit with Rio is joyous and heartwarming, bringing smiles and happiness to many of the residents … and also to us.

Having seen how my sister loved to have therapy dogs visit her when she was in the nursing home, I can appreciate how much people would love to see a dog or other pet. Having gone through this process has made me realize how honored I am to have my partnership with Rio as my best friend and a therapy dog team … and how much I will miss having a dog by my side someday when I am ill or too elderly to have a dog anymore.

I had heard about therapy dog work years ago and saw therapy dogs in the hospitals and nursing homes when I spent time with Mom and Pat, but it never occurred to me that Rio and I were capable of doing something like this. It was only because the American Kennel Club and Dog Scouts of America listed therapy dog work in their list of activities that this activity entered my mind, and gave me the idea that we might be able to do this. I thank them very much for this opportunity to do such honorable and heartwarming work, and for the very important role they have played in our lives.

This has been the most rewarding of all our endeavors, and Rio and I highly recommend the opportunity to other dog owners, and owners of other animals, to become a therapy animal team with your pet if it works for you both.

CHAPTER 43

A Day At The Nursing Home

"The meaning of life is to find your gift. The purpose of life is to give it away."

—*William Shakespeare*

One day, I woke up to the gentle nudging of my foot by my Rio. Odd, my phone alarm had not gone off. Maybe I forgot to set it? More peculiar though, I wondered how Rio knew to wake me up two minutes before my alarm.

I was off from work that day and had told him the night before, "Rio, tomorrow we are going to see Carrie," as I do when we are going to visit the nursing home together as a certified therapy dog team. It was as if Rio understood and remembered what I had said to him the night before, and from some sort of internal clock, knew it was time to get up. He nudged me again to say, "Let's go Mum, it's getting late and we have a lot to do!"

We started the day as usual, with a head and back scratch, long belly rub, and four-paw massage. Then I got dressed and took Rio and Romeo for our morning walk, which I love, because it is a beautiful start to every morning. I love seeing the sun rise, breathing the fresh morning air, and hearing the beautiful birds and other nature sounds.

"It joyfully wakens my mind and gets my legs and blood moving," I say.

After our walk, the boys ate their breakfast, then Rio and I left for the nursing home.

We looked forward to visiting everyone, especially Mr. B., a very kind elderly gentleman who was bedridden and had lost his eyesight and most of his hearing. Although I did not know much about him, he seemed so gentle, wise, and worldly, as if he had traveled a lot and understood life.

Whenever Rio and I entered his room with one of the activities team from the nursing home, Mr. B. was listening to books on tape. The activities assistant would gently touch his hand, and he would always be startled, having been caught up in another world with his book.

"Who is it? What do you want?"

The activities assistant would say loudly, so he could hear, "Mr. B., Rio's here! It's Rio, the therapy dog!"

There was always a moment of silence, then Mr. B. would smile cheek to cheek and say loudly, "It's Rio! Oh, Rio's here! Come here Rio, I want to pet you. Thank you for coming to see me, Rio. I am so happy you are here."

Rio knew how much Mr. B. enjoyed touching and petting him and how important his visit was. At each visit, Rio walked up to Mr. B.'s side and gently placed his head on the side of the bed so Mr. B. could pet him. We visited week after week, and loved to see Mr. B. and make him happy, if only for a short time. How he loved our visits.

One day the activities director told me that at Mr. B's monthly family-status meeting with staff at the nursing home, they always asked him what his favorite event or activity was that month. She said his answer was always, "Rio visits." He has not been the only resident to say this.

We were looking forward to seeing Mr. B. He had been in the hospital for a couple of weeks, but he should be back now.

We made our rounds on each floor of the nursing home, with Rio cheering up all the animal lovers, making new friends, and getting lots of love, pets, and scratches. Rio is a friendly, but polite and good-natured gentleman, and he has a way of winning people's hearts over, even those who were never animal lovers. He greatly enjoys all the love, attention and scratches from everyone he visits.

We did a short dance for some of the residents who were watching Lawrence Welk reruns on television. While I sang along with the activities assistant and some of the residents to *Sentimental Journey*, Rio and I did synchronized spins together, then I walked forward and he backed up. Then he walked through my legs as I did some slow dance moves. We all had good fun, the residents so loved watching Rio dance!

We walked down each hallway, with Rio peeking his head into each room to find more fans interested in seeing him. He had many takers and enjoyed all the attention he received. Rio knew which of the four hallways to walk down next on each floor, and he knew when we were done with the floor, and led us to the elevator.

The residents enjoyed seeing both of us, but the highlight of the visit was always seeing Rio, the star of the team. He made them laugh and smile with his human-like behaviors and expressions. They especially love when he kissed them. Because he is stingy with giving kisses, they felt blessed when he chose them to be the lucky recipient of a kiss that day.

We finally arrived at Mr. B.'s hallway. I asked if he was back from the hospital and doing any better.

"We are so sorry. Mr. B. returned to the nursing home earlier in the week, but passed away suddenly just a few days ago."

I know I should not get emotionally attached to any of the residents, but how could I not? I was very sad to have missed seeing dear Mr. B. one last time, and it was too late to say good-bye to a very special person. Not getting to say good-bye to Mr. B gave me a flashback from nearly 10 years before, when I was too late to say goodbye to someone else very dear, my sister Pat. It brought back a lot of memories and deep sadness that I may never get over.

CHAPTER 44

Romeo, Romeo, Where Are You?

"Farewell happy fields, where joy forever dwells."

—*John Milton, Paradise Lost*

I needed a vacation. It had been a very stressful and depressing time for me since Pat and Mom passed, and so emotionally-draining while cleaning out and selling Mom's house. It was about six years since our last vacation; Joe had since retired and was spending a lot more time at home.

So, we planned a trip of a lifetime, a few weeks in Southeast Asia.

We looked forward to the trip so much, to seeing many things we had never seen before, wonderfully exotic people, beautiful temples, and tasty new foods. It was important to us too that while we were away our beloved dogs should have an equally good time. We considered putting them in the kennel around the corner from us, which takes very good care of them.

Alternatively, I wondered if we should board them, as so many of my friends do, with one of our instructors. Immediately coming to mind was our sheep herding instructor, Gene, who owns the beautiful sheep farm where Rio and Romeo take lessons frequently. Gene and Teri often board dogs, in addition to providing training. I thought Rio and Romeo got along well with them and would have a lot of fun staying there, so I made arrangements for them to do so.

What could be better for two herding dogs than running around free together on dozens of acres of farmland amongst sheep? Plus, there were about a dozen other dogs to play with, ducks, chickens, horses … we thought they would have a fantastic time. I also made arrangements for them to have sheep herding lessons a few times per week. I joked with Gene that they would be all trained by the time we came home and ready for the next sheep herding trials.

I dropped Rio and Romeo off the evening before we left on our trip, right after dinner. Rio is not happy at first when I leave him for boarding, and usually will not eat for a day or two. I wanted him to have a full belly for that evening, so fed them both before I drove the hour to Gene and Teri's.

I had prepared extra special home-cooked meals for them, featuring different meats and vegetables. I also packed their favorite treats in bags for Teri and Gene to give to them. I wanted to be totally prepared for anything, so I created a folder of information about them, though I hoped it would not be needed. I included copies of vaccination and veterinarian reports, with a summary for each dog that I had typed up, including their habits and health information.

I provided our daily contact and hotel information, emergency contact information for family and friends in the United States, and for us in each country on our trip. Not that they would need it, but I also provided microchip information and a recent photo of the boys, and Teri and I set up the Viber email app on my phone so we could keep in touch frequently at no charge.

I stayed a little while at Gene and Teri's house with Rio and Romeo, as I wanted the boys to settle in. After a while, we gave them their favorite chewy snacks. Romeo opted to circle the outskirts of the room to check out his new surroundings. Rio did the same, sniffing everything thoroughly, but finally settling down on the rug with one of the chewies. I stayed until the boys both settled, then said goodnight, kissing and hugging them. Oh, how we would miss them!

We went to sleep that evening in a house that was very empty without Rio and Romeo. We hoped they were adjusting well. Waking very early the next day, we finished packing and left early for JFK airport.

Our flight to Myanmar was uneventful, and Myanmar, a country which had recently eased travel restrictions, welcomed us with open arms. It was a fabulous trip with wonderful people, sightseeing, accommodations, and food. What a magnificent country to see!

I emailed Teri daily to make sure the boys were doing well. We were advised that they were. After a few more days, Joe asked me to have trust in them and stop emailing them every day.

"They are professionals and board dogs all the time — they know what they are doing, so leave them alone," he said.

So I did.

"I will contact them after the weekend," I said.

We loved our magical week-long journey in Myanmar. We had a very knowledgeable and friendly guide, and our small tour group was very nice, with all of us quickly becoming good friends.

We had an introduction to Buddhism, the colorful Myanmar/Burmese culture, and the fascinating history of the country. We were in awe of beautiful temples and stupas during the day and at sunrise and sunset, learned about some of their beautiful art, and saw demonstrations of artists making lacquerware, sand paintings and carved petrified wood. And we enjoyed lots of very good fresh food! Last, but not least, we enjoyed meeting many of their lovely, always happy and smiling, friendly people.

One morning, we had an enjoyable walk through an old marketplace, accompanied by young college students who shared their dreams and aspirations with us. We admired their enthusiasm, intelligence, and genuine kind-heartedness and enjoyed speaking with them. They were curious about us as American foreigners, so we shared some of our life experiences with them. In parting, we encouraged them to follow their dreams, because with hard work and determination, they can come true. We wished them well with their life goals.

Every moment in Myanmar was magical. It was wonderful to see the sites that were written and sung about so many years ago by so many, including Rangoon (now Yangon) and the Ayerwaddy River, and it was exciting to travel the Road to Mandalay. Both of us felt sad when it was time to leave Myanmar. We went on to spend a couple of lovely days in exotic Thailand, then arrived in Laos, looking forward to our tour there.

It was time to follow-up on the boys. Upon arriving to the hotel that evening, I emailed Teri. She replied quickly that Rio was okay and finally eating better. I was glad Rio was eating better, but thought that was odd as Rio usually adjusts in a day or two after we leave, then eats fine. It was over a week now. Odd too, there was no mention of Romeo.

I replied, specifically asking how Romeo was. Viber advised that Teri was reading my email, but I did not get an immediate reply. A half-hour went by, still nothing.

"Something is wrong. Teri is not replying," I said to Joe.

I immediately called Gene and Teri.

I received the worst news — Romeo had run away! Romeo ran away about five days after we left, and had now been gone eight days.

Strong-minded Romeo apparently decided he had had enough of the vacation gig and it was time to go home. Being a very smart dog, I envisioned during the first few days at Gene and Teri's he would have carefully examined the fences, looking for an escape route, and quickly figured out his escape plan. One morning, after Teri left for work, Gene let Rio and Romeo outside for a potty break. Romeo promptly turned to Rio and said, "Sorry Rio, I'm out of here. I'm going home. You're on your own. Good luck."

Romeo busted through two fences and ran off, never looking back. As timid as he was, he was still a German Shepherd, and that comes with a confidence and intelligence that told him he would surely be able to find home, and us.

Off he went, not realizing Joe and I were half a world away!

Gene and Teri had put some of my home-cooked food outside for Romeo in the hopes of attracting him, but he was not coming back, not even to be with his best buddy Rio. He was done with the farm.

Gene and Teri were so upset that Romeo had run away. He was under their care, and being very responsible, they did all they could to get him back. Indeed, they did. They were very thorough and organized, and quickly set up a command station at their home ready with computers, home phone, and cell phones. They created a Facebook page for Romeo titled *Help Us Find Romeo,* and posted information and regular updates about Romeo on over half a dozen local Facebook pages for lost pets.

They even called the local and State Police to advise that Romeo was missing. They asked them to please call if someone phoned in a bear-sighting in the area, because Romeo is big and black and can look like a bear.

Gene and Teri created missing dog flyers for stores and telephone poles, and mobilized dozens of volunteers to post the flyers throughout the local towns where there had been Romeo sightings. Volunteers showed up quickly, perhaps totaling over 200 at some point, and posted flyers and performed other tasks. Some volunteers were devoted to driving around looking for Romeo for hours on end in areas where he had been recently sighted.

Many calls, emails, and texts about Romeo sightings came in, and Gene and Teri promptly responded to everything, rushing out to look for Romeo in the hope they would get there in time.

Many local residents made their properties available to the search team, and new volunteers appeared daily offering to help. A very nice lady was on her way to buy carpeting when she heard that a dog named Romeo was missing. She immediately postponed her shopping, and everything else in her life, to diligently driving around searching for Romeo until the search ended. We thank you from our hearts, dear dog lover. The love and caring that absolute strangers showed for a scared, missing dog was overwhelming. Thank you to all of you, from my heart.

One day, a woman called in saying she was stopped in traffic when she saw a large black dog run from one side of the road to the other, weaving through the cars. She thought the dog was then hit by a car. A firefighter, hearing of this, volunteered his time to look for the possibly injured Romeo using his heat-seeking equipment. He did not find an injured Romeo, which was a wonderful sign, raising everyone's hopes that he was not injured or worse. Quickly, everyone in the neighboring towns seemed to know about Romeo and be on the lookout for him. But the days kept passing, and still, no Romeo. Was his time and luck running out?

Then one day, a wonderful rescue group, Eleventh Hour Rescue, the group from which we had rescued Shaman years ago, contacted Teri and volunteered to help. Eleventh Hour has professional trappers who are very knowledgeable about dogs and have had a lot of success locating and capturing lost dogs. They committed to Gene and Teri that they would do their best to locate Romeo and get him home. Everyone hoped Eleventh Hour would catch Romeo.

Eleventh Hour showed up every day to continue their very organized search. They enlisted a very nice man and his tracking dog to help with the search, and using the scent from Romeo's bed, he and his dog confirmed that the dog spotted in a cornfield 10 miles from Gene and Teri's farm was indeed Romeo.

It was hard to believe Romeo could have safely traveled so far —10 miles — across so many busy roads. But Romeo has a very large stride and is a fast runner, and apparently, is more street-smart and lucky than we all thought.

Gene assured us they were doing everything possible to find Romeo and get him back before we returned. He told us that people called them every day to advise of Romeo sightings, so they were confident he was okay and they would get him back soon.

He told us that they did not tell us he had run away because they did not want to ruin our long-awaited trip of a lifetime. Gene assured me, "We are doing everything we know of to get him home."

I ended the call with Gene and broke out in tears, so worried about Romeo.

I knew we had to leave for home right away, so I asked Joe to find our tour guide.

"Joe, we have to go home and find Romeo. Please find Zhou. We need his help right away, please."

Joe agreed. Romeo is a family member to us, but we were even more concerned because he is an innocent, naïve, sweet soul who had no idea where he was, could not read signs, and could not ask for help. We felt so bad for Romeo and could not imagine how frightened he must be, alone in a remote farm area he did not know.

I knew that although some of the best professional trappers in the state were trying to locate Romeo, the chances of them catching him were slim to none. Romeo is very timid and probably would never come to anyone who called him but us. He had not been socialized by his owner-breeder when in his most critical formative months, then he was given up to the rescue, which in itself had to have been a very frightening event for him.

Since rescuing Romeo when he was one-year-old, it has taken us years to build up a strong trusting relationship with him. Romeo was not going to warm up to anyone and just run up to them, even if they had his favorite food in their hands. I also had a difficult time believing that such a smart German Shepherd would easily be trapped, even by professionals. I believed he would be very suspicious of a trap or crate-like object. The trappers would have to be extraordinarily clever to catch Romeo.

CHAPTER 45

The Long Road Home

*"We often do not appreciate what we have until
we lose it."*

—Joni

There was no question that we had to go home on the first available flight — no hesitation at all. We had to leave as fast as we could to find Romeo and bring him home.

As Joe sought out our guide, I went online to locate the Facebook page Gene and Teri had created for Romeo. I quickly shared that information to my Facebook page, begging for anyone near the area where he was seen to please look out for him. My very good friend Athena (back in the States) immediately responded and offered Gene and Teri her assistance.

Joe found our guide, and we canceled the trip and made flight arrangements to get home to New Jersey. Zhou was very supportive and helpful, having owned a dog, too.

Booking a flight at the last minute does not get you a reasonable airfare. We later learned that our "all inclusive" travel insurance covered not even a penny for the flight and our canceled trip, because runaway dog emergencies were not covered by the insurance.

Romeo is our best buddy, along with Rio, so money was not a consideration. We could only imagine how frightened Romeo must be, and felt so much love and concern for him, knowing that all he wanted to do was go home and be with us. He needed us as soon as possible. We prayed that he would be safe and we would not be too late.

Poor darling Romeo.

"Please hang in there, boy," I prayed.

We arranged to leave on the first flight out. Unfortunately, there were no direct flights, our only option was to fly from Laos to Thailand, then to Hong Kong, then Newark Airport, with layovers in each country.

During the long flights and layovers, all we could do was think of Romeo and how he must be frightened out of his mind, and how upset Rio must be, thinking of how his buddy suddenly ran off and left him all alone at the farm. We prayed for them both.

We were so worried about sweet, innocent Romeo by himself in some unfamiliar field somewhere. He was alone, running scared in places he had never been before, with no food or water except what he could find in the wild.

We prayed he would not be hit by a car, and hoped that our safety training while taking him for walks and leading him off the road when a car approached had taught him something. It was horrifying to think of, but we hoped no one would think he was a black bear and shoot him. All we could do was pray for Romeo to be safe and hang in there until we could find him and get him home safely.

Not surprisingly, we were beside ourselves. The long flights, layovers, and anticipation were daunting. To ease our tension we chatted with fellow travelers, and they all wished us good luck. I could not speak without getting teary-eyed.

While waiting for one of our connecting flights, a very nice young Asian lady gave me a beautiful red elephant keychain for good luck. A very big thank you and hugs to you, my dear friend with a beautiful heart, and to everyone who helped us on our way — you helped get us through this. We thank you from our hearts forever. I will never forget your kindness and generosity. And I will always treasure your gift of your elephant keychain — a good luck charm. Thank you dear friend, I hope our paths cross again at a happy time.

On our final long, 18-hour flight home, I thought of our lessons learned and noted that we had been unlucky with this and our prior vacation. For this trip, we had been so happy that we were finally going on another vacation. It was six years from the last vacation we had taken, right after Mom had passed away, that had ended sadly.

At that time, I had been clearing out over 50 years of memories from Mom's house, as my brother arranged its sale. I was emotionally drained and needed a break, so off Joe and I went with Massachusetts Audubon into the heart of Borneo's rainforests. We had a remarkable trip seeing orangutans, hornbills and other birds, proboscis monkeys, pythons, and so many other species.

Arriving back home, we sat on our deck in the back-yard at midnight to catch up on our emails. We expected nothing earth-shattering, nothing exciting.

Instead, we were shocked to learn that my youngest and very dear cousin, Janie, had committed suicide while we were in Borneo. It was horrible. She suffocated and drowned herself in her bathroom, believing no one cared for her. But everyone did. She was beautiful and such an angel. Now she was gone.

The entire family was devastated by the loss of Janie. It had taken a long time for me to even think about taking another vacation after that. Nothing interested me. Finally, I got the spark for another trip, and we booked this trip to Myanmar, Thailand, Laos, Cambodia and Vietnam.

I prayed that this trip would not also end with disaster.

CHAPTER 46

The Cornfields

*"When missing you, every moment feels like
an eternity."*

—*Joni*

We arrived home near midnight, and immediately called Gene and told him we would drive up that night. Gene told us there was little chance, if any, of finding Romeo at night, so we agreed to wait until morning. We tried to get a few hours of sleep, but all we could do was think of Romeo, scared and all alone somewhere in a cornfield.

Sunday morning finally came. Our emotions ran high, first with fear, then optimistically with hope of getting Romeo back home. I packed some of Romeo's favorite food and treats, and we were up at Gene and Teri's farm before sunrise, ready to search for our missing boy.

Rio was overjoyed to see us. He was so clearly upset that Romeo had run away. He knew something was wrong, but always being a good trooper, he had been

251

a very obedient boy the entire time, listening to Gene and Teri.

I immediately hugged and kissed precious Rio. He jumped on me, put his paws around me in a hug, kissed me, and kissed me some more.

Then staring at me and looking very serious, Rio began talking to me — just like Charlie Brown's Snoopy does in the television shows. He made a lot of emotional, "wah-wah," sounds, like he was conveying a very important message to me.

I understood his message right away.

Rio said, "Mum, Romeo ran away, and we have to go find him. We have to hurry, because he's been gone a long time."

After more kisses from Rio, and waiting for direction from Gene and Teri, I started to feed Rio breakfast. Halfway through, the phone rang — a young mother, always on the lookout for that sweet boy named Romeo, had just sighted him in a cornfield while driving her son to soccer practice.

Romeo was in the cornfield 10 miles away!

Joe, Rio, and I jumped into Joe's car and Teri into hers. We followed Teri to the cornfield, a place where Romeo had been seen before, but as we expected, he was already gone. Romeo can cover a lot of ground quickly with his long, German Shepherd stride.

Teri received several other calls about Romeo sightings soon after, so we drove to other nearby open fields, cornfields, and a residential neighborhood, but no luck.

We were very disheartened. So close, but no luck.

However, we were very happy that Romeo was alive. At least, we hoped it was him who everyone was sighting.

At a Veterans of Foreign Wars building near a wildlife rehabilitation center nearby we met Terry, who had just arrived from Eleventh Hour. It was now late morning. Terry told us that Eleventh Hour was trying to get hold of an extra-large crate they could use to try to catch Romeo. On a hunch, she suggested Joe and I go to one of the cornfields where Romeo had been seen frequently. She said we should walk around the field and quietly call Romeo, then sit and wait for a while to see if he would appear. She hoped this might flush Romeo out.

We immediately drove to the cornfield, then walked through the surrounding wooded area (full of wild rose bushes and brambles with lots of thorns) to the cornfield. Splitting up, I walked for several minutes and dropped some of Romeo's favorite treats that I had brought with us, and wiped some corn stalks with his favorite coconut oil. I hoped he would smell these scents and know that we were there to get him and take him home. Then I sat down on the ground for a while and softly called for Romeo.

Joe walked the perimeter of the cornfield, looking for a sign of Romeo. After about an hour, he joined me. He had seen large dog footprints in the dried mud and took a photo with his phone to show me. Both of us believed it was Romeo's large snowshoe footprints.

We called out for Romeo, but he did not come. We sat for a while longer, but still Romeo did not appear. Calling Teri to see what we should do, she suggested we take a quick lunch break and pick up some supplies for Eleventh Hour that they would need for the search that afternoon. We went to the food store and did as she suggested, then regrouped with Teri and Terry.

To our dismay, they explained that the cornfield where we had sat, where Romeo had been seen frequently, would be plowed to the ground on Tuesday or Wednesday. They said we must try to get Romeo before then because the plowing would likely scare him away, plus he would have no place to hide with the corn stalks gone.

Eleventh Hour wanted to try a couple of things, though they did not think they would have any success, but there was nothing else to try. First, they wanted to set up a trail camera with food that Romeo likes in the field that we were just in. I gave them some of Romeo's favorite food and treats, and Eleventh Hour returned to the cornfield to set up the trail camera and food and returned shortly. Someone at Eleventh Hour began remotely monitoring the trail camera's live feed.

We waited, not so patiently.

Soon, Terry began receiving live feeds on her cell phone of the video camera activity in the field. At first there was nothing. No Romeo.

About thirty minutes or so later, Terry received a video showing Romeo's arrival on the trail, and showing him starting to eat the food! He ate everything. Great news! It was the first time Joe and I actually saw Romeo since he ran away — he was alive!

What should we do next? The crate option was out. Eleventh Hour confirmed they could not get the large crate that evening.

They suggested we try Plan B as the last resort today, but warned us they had very little hope of success. They wanted me or Joe to take Rio into the cornfield where Romeo was just seen, in the slim hope that Romeo would come to us. They told us not to get our hopes up at all, because it would be *one chance in a hundred* that this would work. They explained that a number of times while trying to recover other runaway dogs, they had sadly watched a scared dog run right over its owner's feet, having no idea it was his owner. That is because runaway dogs, after being many days in a place they are not familiar with, are in survival mode, like a feral animal, so are not thinking normally. They warned that Romeo might see us and run away from us, not realizing who we are.

We had to take that chance.

I nominated Joe for the duty of going into the field with Rio. I thought that was the best option, because I was the one who had dropped Romeo off at the farm. If Romeo saw me coming towards him, I thought there was a good chance he might think I had come to take him back there. We could not afford to take that risk.

Tag — Joe and Rio were it.

Suddenly, Teri's phone rang.

A new spotting of Romeo!

Sighters had just seem Romeo at the corner of the cornfield property where he was just seen on the trail camera!

Into our cars we went and off to the cornfield. The 10-minute drive seemed like an eternity.

Rounding the corner of the cornfield, we saw the sighters in their cars parked on the opposite side of the road. Teri asked them to stay put so Romeo would not spook from so much activity.

As we started to park, Romeo popped his head out of the dense wooded area several hundred feet up the road. We were thrilled to finally see Romeo in real life — now we truly knew he was alive!

He stood at the edge of the wooded area, watching our cars. This was the dense area of deciduous trees and scrub Joe and I had walked through earlier to get into the cornfield.

Joe could not contain himself, so opened his car door. Despite Joe being quiet and slow in his movements, Romeo heard him and quickly ducked back into the wooded area. Romeo did not know who we were yet, and clearly did not trust to wait and find out.

Teri asked Joe to be quiet, but to quickly take Rio into the cornfield where we'd sat earlier. Joe got out of the car, leashed Rio, and together they walked across the road towards the cornfield.

Teri jumped into the driver's seat and drove Joe's car forward toward where we had seen Romeo enter the woods. She started to back up the car and looked in the rearview mirror to see if any traffic was coming, then yelled out, puzzled, "Joe's coming out of the field already ... what's wrong?"

Then joyously, "And he has two dogs!!!"

It happened so quickly. Joe and Rio were suddenly back on the street in front of us with Romeo on lead and safe. We pulled the car up to Joe and the boys, so happy.

The sighters came to us as well, then Gene drove up. We were all so happy and relieved, many of us in tears.

I quickly put Romeo into Joe's car so he could not escape, but he was overjoyed to be back with us and was not going anywhere. He was not going to let us out of his sight. He stuck his head out of the car and gave Joe and me dozens of juicy kisses.

CHAPTER 47

Welcome Home!

"Luck is what happens when preparation meets opportunity."

— Seneca

omeo! Romeo! We are so happy to have you back! Romeo, thank goodness you are okay! We were so relieved and grateful that Romeo was back safe with us.

Joe then told us what had happened. He walked with Rio through the wooded area toward the cornfield, calling out Romeo's name softly. Suddenly, Romeo popped his head around the corner of the field, looking cautiously at Rio, who was in the lead, then Joe. Joe stood still, softly calling out Romeo's name.

"Romeo … Romeo … good boy, Romeo. Rio's here, Romeo. Joanie's home. Let's go home Romeo," and all kinds of things he always says to Romeo. Romeo took a few cautious steps forward, then stopped, looking at Joe and Rio.

RIO ♥ A LOVE STORY

Rio recognized his buddy Romeo and started moving toward Romeo to say, "Hello — thank goodness you're back!"

Suddenly, Romeo recognized Rio and began trotting up to him. The two boys met and started kissing (a "doggie kissfest," Joe said), wagging their tails in absolute delight. Who says dogs do not have feelings? They were so clearly ecstatic to see each other.

Then Romeo recognized Joe and ran up to him and started kissing him too, and while Joe hugged Romeo, he quickly slipped his collar onto him. That all happened in the time it took for Teri to get in the car and start turning the car around, just a minute or two.

Relief flooded through us, we were ecstatic to have Romeo back! The poor boy, we had no idea what he had been through. Oh Romeo, Romeo, we love you, Romeo. Welcome home, dear boy!

We were so grateful for everyone's help and thanked them profusely. It had truly been an emotional roller-coaster ride, from exhaustion fueled by stress and our fear that something awful might happen to Romeo, then full circle to the ultimate joy of getting him back!

We recapped quickly, all agreeing it was awesome that Romeo came to Rio and Joe so quickly, something that was given a chance of one in a hundred. We agreed it was helpful for Romeo that Joe and I had walked the cornfield and dropped treats, leaving our scent there with that of his favorite treats and coconut oil, followed by putting some of his favorite food and treats down for the trail camera. It may well be that after we left our scents in the cornfield earlier that morning, Romeo smelled them and thought of us.

The consensus was that Romeo smelled the familiar food scents and had time to register them, likely recognizing his favorite food and treats that he gets at home when doing nose work, tracking, and other activities, and must also have recognized our scent in the field.

Perhaps by smelling those scents he was taken a few levels down from his feral mode — the survival mode he was in that would normally not enable him to recognize some of his favorite scents and people. Once that happened, he returned closer to a state of mind where he was able to recognize Joe and Rio as friends, not strangers, and that is probably why he ran up to them so quickly.

Romeo may have been waiting, hoping and praying for Joe, Rio, and me to appear. We believed that Romeo's nose work and tracking skills enabled him to instinctively use his scenting ability in the wild. Although Romeo is too nervous to focus during an odor recognition test, I firmly believe the training Romeo and I have done together helped get him back that day. Thank goodness for nose work and tracking training!

All were exhausted, especially Romeo, Gene and Teri. We went back to the farm, thanked Gene and Teri, gathered some of our things and went home to hug the boys and give them a very special dinner. We were one happy family, together again. All was well.

Romeo was in high spirits, but physically, we had a lot of work to do. He had lost 10 pounds and was now about 90 pounds. He was quite a mess too, and needed a bath, having been in the woods and fields for 10 days. Burs were embedded all through his long coat from the wildflowers in the fields, and were deeply tangled in his undercoat. He had gouges on his face, head and neck from wild roses and blackberry brambles in the woods, and he had ticks, hundreds of them. Although we pulled almost 100 ticks off Romeo that night and the next day, when we took him to the vet and groomer they removed well over another 100 ticks.

Because we did not know exactly where Romeo had been, what he ate and drank, or if he had any encounters with other animals, wild or domestic, our vet gave us a number of antibiotics to give him.

The groomer bathed Romeo thoroughly, and he looked beautiful once more. He was feeling much better, having been groomed, well fed, and with all those ticks removed. His happy demeanor told us he was thrilled to be home.

As closure to this very difficult adventure, Teri, a dear person and so very smart, started an online GoFundMe page to benefit Eleventh Hour Rescue, intended to raise enough money to buy an extra-large crate or two just in case another large dog like Romeo runs away and gets lost. We were all paying it forward. Over $2,000 was raised for Eleventh Hour Rescue.

Thank you again, Eleventh Hour Rescue, for all your amazing efforts in rescuing Romeo.

How is Romeo today? He had a small setback with this incident, but is now doing very well. He has gained back most of the confidence he lost, and we continue to socialize him and take him to training classes. Joe and I take him for long walks in safe city areas, sit outside at dog-friendly restaurants and go to dog-friendly shops. We try to get him to mingle as much as possible with people, and when appropriate, with other dogs.

I have been taking Romeo for nose work, Parkour, and therapy dog training. We hope Romeo, like Rio, can become a therapy dog someday.

Before this incident, Romeo was to the point of actually walking up to people we met on the street to say "Hi!" After some work, he is nearing that confidence level again. We are happy he is returning to his new normal.

We are so glad to have Romeo back and to resume our lives together, and hope to spend long healthy lives with both Rio and Romeo, as they bring us much joy and a new appreciation for being together. We give our thanks every day.

CHAPTER 48

Who Is Training Who?

"Enjoy every moment — we don't know how many moments we have left."

—Joni

Feeling so blessed after finding Romeo and getting him home safely, we were very glad to be home to enjoy the simple but rich things in life, like being together and our morning walks. I walk nearly every morning, with the only exceptions being if I have to get up really early for work or a trial or if the weather is too hot or raining.

You never know what we will come across on our walks, or before!

One day, before we had even decided to go for a walk, we discovered that Rio and Romeo are co-conspirators. No kidding. They manipulate us!

Joe and I were busy at home; I was on the computer and Joe was watching television. Suddenly, Romeo went up to the couch and started staring at Joe with his big, beautiful brown eyes. Joe did not acknowledge him at first, waiting to see what he would do next.

Romeo waited a minute, then began to bark softly.

Joe looked up, then Romeo stepped backwards. Joe stood up.

Romeo then turned around, enticing Joe to move toward the kitchen door. Joe followed him, wondering what he was up to, and was amazed.

Rio was standing in a nice stack at the kitchen door, nose pointed outside. He obviously wanted to go outside for some reason, maybe to do his business or play, but had been totally silent. He clearly had not been silent with Romeo, however. The two of them had worked as a team to encourage Joe to open the door! Rio was happy that Joe had arrived, at Romeo's request, and began wagging his tail.

Joe let the two of them outside. What a well-trained human!

∞

Rio charms me pretty much no matter what he does. He is just beautiful, and I love him. He makes me laugh, and I love to watch him, to see him learn and discover new things, probably the way any mom feels about her kids. I love to see the expression on his face when a lightbulb goes on as he realizes he understands something new I am teaching him.

On a particularly brisk morning we went for a fast walk, me thinking we would walk through the neighborhood and add another mile toward Rio's next Dog Scout title.

As we approached our neighbor's yard, Rio spotted an unsuspecting squirrel who had his back to us. The squirrel did not see or smell us, he just went on his way, doing what squirrels do best — foraging for food.

Rio is not a killer. Rather, he is a lover, and loves to say, "Hi!" and make friends with every animal he meets. Rio has stood nose-to-nose with horses, sheep, a camel, caged rabbits and birds, crated cats, fish in a tank, and face-to-face with a baby fox outside our sliding glass door, always with his tail wagging. Most of the time, the other animals reciprocate in some way, sensing that Rio is truly a gentle spirit who wants to be friends and means no harm.

Rio was enchanted and curious, watching the back of the squirrel as it foraged for acorns in the grass under a very old and very large oak tree. The perimeter of the base of the tree was about four-and-one-half feet wide, and it was very healthy, with many leaves and acorns.

The squirrel finally heard Rio and ran behind the tree to hide. Rio stalked the squirrel, not so much in prey mode, but rather with his tail wagging, happy and excited to perhaps meet a new friend. Rio went around the left of the tree, as I have taught him to do when doing a "Go Around" for rally and Parkour. He went "around" to the right, then again to the left, all the while sniffing the tree and the ground, following the scent of the squirrel. He sniffed all the nooks and crannies of the tree and its large roots, thinking the squirrel may have somehow gone inside the tree. It was amazing to see him work with his nose and observe his genuine curiosity about where the squirrel went.

Rio again went around the tree to the left, then to the right, left, right, left, right. He was so cute with his tail up in the air and his face showing such child-like curiosity. I could not help but smile and chuckle. I pointed "up" where the squirrel must have gone (but I did not see him). Rio did not quite get that concept right then, although he does understand heights. He even knows that we are on the second or third floor when we visit the nursing home and avoids getting anywhere near the windows on the higher floors, being afraid of heights. I find that remarkable.

We did not see the squirrel anymore, so began to walk farther up the street, getting about 20 feet when Rio heard something. We both turned around to see the squirrel jump off the tree to the ground to start grazing again. Rio was mesmerized once more, and tried to approach it, but the squirrel would not let us get anywhere close to him. Nor would I let Rio get close to the squirrel, because the squirrel could possibly bite and hurt him, though it would likely run away first if it could. All this while on my neighbor's property, who probably thinks we are both a bit crazy!

CHAPTER 49

Rio's Health

"Grow old with me ... the best is yet to be."

—*Robert Browning*

Belgian Tervuren can be susceptible to certain illnesses (as are other breeds), with some suffering from epilepsy and seizures, while some get stomach cancer, like Marly.

I was very upset when Rio had a small seizure at about the age of two. It lasted less than a minute, but felt like an eternity. Although it appeared to be very mild, not a violent seizure like many dogs have, it was nonetheless very disturbing to me.

Since then, and up until about a year ago, the seizures occurred once in a while, not every month, but when they did it was usually somewhere near a full moon, and usually at night. Luckily, they did not stop Rio from living a very happy, active life. We learned to minimize them and their occurrences with diet and supplements; we worked around them.

Rio knew when a seizure was coming on and would become anxious, then look for me. Rio found me and sometimes just wanted to be held, other times he laid on his side. He was always fully conscious and knew something wrong was happening. He tensed up sometimes, to varying degrees, and at times drooled a little, and early on, his feet would move a bit, like he was taking baby steps in the air. My goal when this happened was to make him know he is a very good boy and that everything was going to be fine.

"Good boy, Rio. You are so good! Everything is good. I love you," I whispered to him, to calm him.

I did not cry, show fear or panic, or raise my voice, because he knows they are negative things, and it would affect him. Sometimes I massaged his ears or body slowly to help calm him.

After the first episode, I took Rio to our conventional veterinarian. When it happened again, he suggested medication. We tried the drug, but noted that each time Rio had a pill he was sluggish and acted strangely right after. I discussed this with our vet, and after much consideration, he decided not to continue with the medication because Rio was not getting severe or frequent seizures.

Wanting to keep track of when the seizures were happening, and what happened before them, I started a journal. I quickly discovered that Rio's seizures mostly occurred just before, on, or right after a full moon. This made sense because of the effect the moon has on water and the tides, and the fact that we are all mostly made up of water.

I did a lot of research on conventional and alternative ways of dealing with seizures. I read that vaccines could have negative effects, like seizures, on some dogs, so I started to get Rio titers in place of vaccinations where we could. A titer is where the vet takes a sample of the dog's blood to test the level of antibodies, as high enough levels to combat the disease tested for means a vaccination is not required at that time.

I took Rio to our alternative medicine vet, who offered liquid herbal drops that minimize the frequency and strength of the seizures. I also improved his diet by transitioning to nearly all organic meats, home-cooked with vegetables. I changed our lifestyle, eliminating chemicals from our environment by replacing all cleaning products with natural ones, buying products where possible with low or no volatile organic compounds, and so on.

I was pleased to see Rio's seizures decrease to very little frequency, and to much less than a minute with very little activity compared to when they first started happening.

Then I discovered CBD oil. That appears to have had a very good effect on Rio. He has not had a seizure, to my knowledge, for almost a year since I started giving him several drops of CBD oil daily.

Importantly, I try to keep Rio happy with a very positive atmosphere and lots of love. We never did let the threat of seizures stop Rio from doing what he wants to do — we went out, stayed busy, and enjoyed life. He always wants to go out to training classes, trials, meet new friends, and go everywhere with us. That is what keeps him happy, which may be part of the cure.

Rio has been very healthy otherwise, but one day, I noticed what I thought was a drop of blood on the floor.

"No, it could not be blood," I said.

Maybe Rio or Romeo cut their foot, so I checked them thoroughly, but did not find a cut or any possible source of bleeding.

More drops of blood appeared around the house here and there. I could not figure out where it was coming from until one morning when Rio was standing next to me on the pale-colored tiled kitchen floor, and I saw a drop of blood fall to the floor from his penis.

At about the same time, I noticed that Rio lost some of his appetite, almost always a sign that something is not right with a dog.

Our vet quickly diagnosed Rio with a swollen prostate gland, and advised that this is common in older dogs and it would be best to have Rio neutered in the next week or so, as that would take care of this problem. It seemed to be an emergency.

I was upset. I could not imagine Rio, my proud show dog and ladies' man, without all his gentlemanly parts. Not to mention that someday, I hoped Kate and Jeff, his breeders, would breed him. Although in reality I knew that would not happen, I still did not want my beloved Rio to lose any of his parts, so I contacted Kate immediately and discussed this dilemma with her.

Kate shared my concerns, and said I should contact my holistic vet to see if she could recommend anything natural. Kate advised that she has friends who had their Belgian dog neutered, and the dog was never the same. He lost his drive and energy to do things, and perhaps went into depression, losing his happy Belgian personality and enjoyment of life.

I did not want this to happen to Rio, so I did my own research. Some articles I read said that all parts of the body serve a purpose, so when one is removed, often the body needs to compensate for its function and goes out of balance, possibly causing other physical or mental health issues. This all made perfect sense to me.

Then I sat back and reasoned, some men in my family have enlarged prostate glands, but not one doctor ever told them to get any part of their body removed because of it! That would not go over too well with men, would it?

Our holistic vet is very good. She practices conventional vet care, but also blends in holistic care, such as herbs, when appropriate. She reviewed the lab report I gave her, smiled, and simply said, "We can give Rio an herb named saw palmetto daily, and that should take care of the problem."

Funny, Joe told me that he took saw palmetto because of the same problem. We started giving Rio a pill in the morning with his meal; the bleeding stopped almost immediately, and his appetite returned fully.

I am amazed at how sometimes certain herbs and vitamins can naturally cure or remedy an ailment, often very quickly. It is curious how so many things that are true natural cures are brushed aside and called old wives' tales or hogwash, yet they really do work. I have read many times, from many sources, that healing is not just about prescription drugs, operations, and radiation.

Rather, from experience, I would say it is important to do your own thorough research to see if there may be alternative, natural ways of handling your health problems, or ways to complement and work with conventional medicine to have the best of both worlds.

I have a number of herbs and kitchen foods I keep on hand for various uses, and I can vouch for certain natural remedy cures as we experienced with my sister's illness, and duplicated later with other relatives. Rio has been on saw palmetto now for more than two years, and all is well.

Other than that, and Lyme disease on rare occasions from the ticks that swarm all over the East Coast, Rio has been a very healthy boy, very happy and energetic, always testing well at the vets. We hope he stays healthy and lives a long healthy life! May God bless you always, Rio!

CHAPTER 50

Super Dogs!

"Dogs come in all shapes and sizes with an enormous variety of skills — what are your dog's best traits?"

—Joni

For some reason that I do not understand, many people often look down on dogs and other animals. The more I learn about dogs, the more I do not think they should be looked down on. We, as humans, may consider ourselves superior to them in many ways, and maybe we are. Yes, we have created the computer and all sorts of technology, cars, airplanes, and all kinds of advanced medical technology, war machines, bombs, and electronics. We can dig up fossil fuels and build plastics and other items from various natural resources, and now we have 3D printing and other incredible things.

But dogs have one-upped us in many ways, and so many of us cannot do without them. Each dog is special, and each breed seems to have its own remarkable abilities.

Dogs have been companions to humans for so very long and have helped us in so many ways.

For example, dogs can be incredible watchdogs and guard dogs, having been protectors of people, babies, homes, farms, and businesses from other people and animals, even from lions and other large predators. Around the world they protect sheep and other animals from predators, including in Africa, where dogs are trained to keep cheetahs away from stock and poachers away from endangered species. Dogs are trained to find illegal ivory shipments in the airports in Africa.

Dogs can herd and protect sheep on their own without their human being on watch. They help with hunting — identifying where the prey is and bringing it back to their humans. They can swim and save people from drowning. Dogs are stars with their superior scenting and tracking abilities and can locate missing persons, both dead and alive. They can sniff out bombs, drugs, and other illegal substances. More and more, dogs are trained to locate invasive species and to protect threatened and endangered species, and can even detect bacteria in beehives, critical to the survival of our precious bee population.

How amazing are the dogs who can tell someone when they should take their pills because their blood pressure is too low, notify parents that their child is about to have a seizure, and dial 911 when their owner needs assistance? Some dogs can detect various cancers in people too, and reportedly are more accurate than some cancer-detecting methods. They are invaluable service dogs to their owners. Some have alerted their owners that there is a gas leak or fire when they are sleeping, and physically pulled people out of dangerous situations. Others have protected injured people in the wild from predators, even keeping them warm in freezing weather situations, barking all the while for assistance.

Therapy dogs, like Rio, can cheer up patients who are in pain or full of anxiety just by showing up and giving them a kiss, reminding them of happy yesterdays when they were younger and may have had a dog, cat, or other pets and loved and had a lot of fun with them.

Dogs have been known to assist children with confidence and speaking issues when no human has had success; some help children excel in reading-assistance classes simply by listening to the child read. Dogs are used in work environments, courtrooms, schools, airports, and other places to cheer up and calm down people of all ages who are under stress from their current situation or just their everyday lives. Emotional-support dogs can give someone with emotional needs the daily assistance they require to function to their best ability, whether they are at work, home, or traveling in a stressful environment.

Dogs, and other animals too, provide so many wonderful talents and abilities naturally that humans cannot. I do not know of anyone who can do what they can do. I do not believe we are better than they, we are just different.

Dogs are really good at what they do — being dogs. They can communicate with you if you let them be happy and relaxed, and if you really try to listen. There are so many good instructors and training books that will help you understand more about what your dog is telling you if you would like to enhance your relationship with your dog or other pet.

As such, I put Rio and Romeo on a pedestal, because they have so many abilities that I do not have and never will, and they can do so many things I cannot. I respect and greatly admire them, and because of that, I believe they respect me even more. They are, simply, magical.

As a responsible dog Mum, all I can do is give Rio and Romeo lots of love, great food, a comfortable home, and hopefully a happy, long, and healthy life. While doing all of this, I try my best to communicate with them, train them, enhance our relationships, and let them enjoy all the dog sports and activities that I can each day to give them a fulfilling life. I believe they know I am trying to do all these things for them and appreciate that.

CHAPTER 51

Smarty Pants!

"Don't underestimate the intelligence of your dog."

—Joni

At some point during our various training classes, quite by accident I discovered the book *Chaser*, which intrigued and inspired me to learn more about dog training and the potential intelligence of dogs, especially my dogs. It is a well-written book by retired professor, John Pilley, who brought a Border Collie puppy into his life. He named her Chaser, and decided to not only have her as a beloved family member, but as an important research subject.

In addition to having a new best friend, Mr. Pilley wanted to expand the amount of research that has been done on dog intelligence. As part of this, he wanted to see how many words he could teach Chaser — both the names of her toys and verbal commands related to them such as "find it." He trained Chaser well, and did a comprehensive research paper about his findings.

Chaser can identify more than 1,000 toys and can find them when directed to do so. When Mr. Pilley obtained a new toy and gave it a name not used on other toys, then placed it among some of Chaser's "known" toys, Chaser differentiated between the known and new toy and identified the new toy. Like most Border Collies, Chaser is very smart and learns quickly. She is very well known for her accomplishments, has her own Facebook page, and has even been on television.

This all made me think deeply that, despite all the things dogs can do for us personally and in society, many of us probably underestimate the intelligence of our dogs. As a result of reading *Chaser*, I got more involved with training my dogs every moment I could, even with very simple things. I started teaching Rio and Romeo more and more valuable obedience commands like stop, stay, and wait, as well as useful words like car and door.

I also taught them fun commands like "I have to go potty," and they continue to lead me to the bathroom faithfully. I have fun at the dog trials Rio and I attend. When we arrive, I show Rio where the human potties are, and identify them as "potty." Later in the day, when I say, "Rio, take me to the potty," he leads the way. This, of course, is followed by my question to Rio, "Do you have to go potty?" which asks if *he* has to go potty.

I greatly surprised one of my friends at the Belgian National when I asked Rio if he had to go potty. She watched curiously as Rio immediately stood up and started leading me through the aisles and dog grooming areas — to the exit door more than 500 feet away! He remembered exactly where it was, from the first moment I had shown him earlier. Rio amazed my friend and me alike.

Another command of important use the boys learned is "around." Not only do I use this in the rally ring, but in Parkour and out in the neighborhood as a practical matter when they are on lead and walk around a tree, telephone pole, or rose bushes. I instruct them to "Go around," and they come back immediately around whatever it is they had gone around. If you've ever found yourself in a tangle with your dog's lead around a pole, you'll know how valuable this instruction is!

To date, Rio knows hundreds and hundreds of words. I have not tried to tally them recently, but a couple of years ago I did a partial tally and he knew well over 300 nouns and verbs. I keep working with both Rio and Romeo daily and see their faces light up in joy whenever they learn another word and we both realize that we continue to better understand one another. They are so happy, and so am I!

To me, no matter what breed a dog is, each dog is like a person. Some are smarter, or perhaps just a bit more attentive than others, just like people. Some are calmer, some cuter, some more active, some more friendly, and some more protective, just like people. They do not speak our language, but they have their own, and their own special talents and skills, most of which we do not have the ability to do.

In addition to all their skills and intelligence, dogs have emotions. Some people still say dogs have no feelings or emotions, yet I have read that this has finally been scientifically proven to be incorrect.

For many years, family and friends told me, "That is only a dog." After I got my first dog, Shaolin, I argued with family against all those statements, having personally experienced the intelligence and emotions that Shaolin, Marly, and all our other dogs have shown.

The dogs I know have feelings, and a lot of them. I do not need a scientific study to confirm the obvious — that Rio, Romeo and my other dogs, to varying degrees, exhibited and have had a multitude of emotions, and more feeling and kindness than many humans I have met.

Rio is my best example, because I have trained extensively with him and have become so close to him that I consider him my soul mate. Rio shows happiness, at various levels. He wags his tail at varying speeds depending on his level of joy. He may wag his tail, like many dogs do, so hard that his body moves with it — the tail wags the dog, so to speak.

Rio often smiles at me, some smiles larger than others, when I rub or scratch his belly or I ask if he wants to go for a walk or ride. Sometimes he is in absolute joy and just stares at me with dreamy eyes, sometimes for minutes, like when I tell him I love him.

When I praise Rio for doing something well, he stands tall, smiles, and his eyes are extra bright, and when I praise him after he does something that has been difficult or challenging for us, he is extra proud. His entire face seems to smile, and he wiggles his entire body while leaning against me.

Rio shows love, especially when he lies by my side and gazes at me for a long time. He shows boundless playfulness when he wants me or Romeo to go outside and play with him. He gets a sparkle in his eye and a smile on his face, and sometimes will whine or bark at me in play, then he will do his "backward Terv slide," where he pounces up and down with both front paws from the right to the left side of me, while moving backward with his back feet, enticing me to join him.

He shows curiosity when confronted with new things that do not scare him, such as when observing a bird feeding on the ground nearby, or a chipmunk passing by him. At other times, he shows some uncertainty or fear, such as when a large clump of snow from a tree above falls next to him, making a loud thump.

Rio has shown embarrassment when he has thrown up some grass or food that did not sit well with him that day, but I reassure him it is okay to throw up without being embarrassed. And he gives me a, "No, it was not me," look when I find my slacks on the floor in the bathroom with all the treats emptied out of their pockets.

"It was Romeo, Mum! Not me!" I knew that it was Romeo. Rio doesn't pick pockets.

Rio showed a clear sense of duty, surprise, and an "oops!" emotion, much to my amazement, at the Belgian Specialty Show in Massachusetts, when he thought he'd missed a command. It was amazing to watch, and although we NQ'd, I could not be disappointed with him. He was trying so hard to be a good boy and do a great job in the ring. My good boy Rio just wanted to please me! Needless to say, we did not get one of the nice specialty ribbons, but I learned a lot about his good character and intelligence that day.

He also gets jealous at times, but in a very cute way. I might be brushing, training, or petting Romeo, and Rio, without exception, comes over to squeeze himself between us so he can get my attention. Sometimes he so wants my attention he will actually squeal and rush over to get between me and Romeo, then he gives me a gentle love nudge, a sweet reminder that I belong to him. And if I start scratching Rio with two hands, then take one hand off to pet Romeo, Rio squeals in jealousy, because he wants all of me.

Rio also has gotten jealous or protective a few times when another intact male has approached us with its owner. Rio nearly always will wag his tail at the approaching dog, but a few times there was something about the other dog that raised Rio's concern. As such, he would not let that dog near me and signaled to me his concern by standing tall and close to my side. His actions caused the other dog to growl and bark at Rio.

Rio feels loyalty and devotion to me. He follows me everywhere and stays by my side, and wants to be with me always. If we are at a trial and I ask someone to hold him for a few minutes so I can walk the rally course, he will stand calmly with that person, but he stares at me the entire time I am in the ring, keeping an eye on me, and making sure I do not leave him.

He also feels sad emotions, being upset, and sometimes even a mild disgust. This happens almost every time I leave to go to work in the morning. He knows my morning work day routine, but hope springs eternal with Rio. He hopes he will go somewhere with me every time I get up from bed and get ready to go out. As I finish readying for work and approach the kitchen door to go down the stairs to the garage, Rio waits patiently, standing right by the door. He looks at me so hopefully and says, "Where are we going today, Mum?"

Too often for him, I say, "I have to go to work today, Rio."

Without fail, Rio looks at me, makes a funny face by scrunching it in disappointment, then sighs, turns, and walks away to flop down on his bed. All this is done with a longing look as he stares at me in the hope that I will change my mind and take him with me. He is obviously frustrated that we are not going someplace.

Rio is also very perceptive, as therapy and service dogs can be. He knows when I am sad or upset and walks up to me smiling, eyes shining, and nudges me while advising me wisely, "Be happy Mum, this too shall pass. You are with me and everything is all right."

Rio is especially amazing at the nursing home where we visit as a certified therapy dog team. There are special moments every time we visit, but one I especially loved was the time when one of the assistant activities directors asked Mr. J. if he would like to see Rio.

Mr. J. was sitting in the hallway in his pajamas and bathrobe, waiting for a nurse to come and help him. He told us, "No, I am not feeling well today."

"Okay, have a nice day Mr. J., please feel better," I said, and started moving on.

Rio had other ideas. He had been watching Mr. J. the entire time and knew exactly what he needed to feel better. Rio stepped forward and nudged Mr. J.'s arm with his nose, looking at him inquisitively.

Mr. J. broke out in a smile, chuckled, and said, "Yes, thank you, Rio. You are such a good boy. Of course, I want to see you. I feel better already. You are truly the best medicine." It was a blessed moment.

Rio does not give out many kisses, but he seems to give them to those who most need them at the nursing home and hospice. So many times he has approached people and given them a quick kiss on their hand or face, as if to say, "Do not worry, I will always love you and be your friend." His powers of perception and ability to give love at the right moment amaze me.

Yes, dogs have emotions, and a lot of them. We just need to take the time to learn how to communicate and understand what they are telling us. A joyful, peaceful, kind and supportive environment helps this to happen.

CHAPTER 52

The Gift

"I feel that someone is always looking out for me."

—Joni

I believe that although many of our loved ones are gone from this Earth in the form that we knew them, they will always be with us, not only in our hearts but watching over us. I have been told by many friends that those we have lost still love us, and at times, send us gifts to help us or simply to remind us of them. Those gifts may come in many different forms and can be very precious.

I thank my sister Pat for the gift of Rio. It has taken me a while to come to this realization, but I believe Pat sent Rio to me, as a priceless life-giving gift from her. Pat always loved dogs and knew how happy they made her. They kept her life complete and happy, and she wanted that for me, too.

Pat sent Rio to me to save my life at a very dark and dangerous time for me. She told me at her darkest time, when she was dying in the hospital, that life is not worth living if you do not feel alive. From wherever she was looking over me, I know she was so sad for me and wanted to help me. I believe Pat wanted to let me know that she, and everyone who has already passed, still loves me and that I am not alone. She wanted to give me back my life, or perhaps to give me a new one, not a sad one with no meaning, but one with real love and excitement, with happy goals and dreams.

I hadn't realized it while she was alive, but Tervs were on Pat's short-list of her favorite dogs. I found her list after she had passed away, while cleaning out Mom's house after Mom had passed too. Pat knew what a tough time I would face after her passing, with Mom to follow, along with other tragedies. Being the ever-caring big sister, she sent me the most special gift of an incredibly kind soul, Rio, knowing that Rio would fill my life with love.

Pat knew that Rio, a show dog, would give me the gift of a new life and open many new doors of adventure. Pat never had the opportunity to show dogs because she had other things to accomplish here on Earth during her short stay. She loved dog shows and wanted me to have the awesome opportunity she never had — to run into the show ring with a gorgeous dog by my side and enjoy every breathless moment that showing a dog offers.

She wanted me to have a very close, most special relationship with an extraordinarily gentle soul, someone who would always adore me and be by my side. Someone with a huge sense of humor who would teach me so much about life, happiness, caring, loyalty, along with comedy, humility, embarrassment, but most of all, eternal, never-ending unconditional love. Someone who would teach me to enjoy life, to live in the "now," and remind me to slow down and savor each moment and appreciate all that I have and once had. And to desire more for myself.

Pat and I, sisters who at times would disagree, but through it all always treasured each other, are still and will forever be connected even though she has passed. Sometimes, I wonder if Pat communicates with me through Rio, reminding me at special times to stop and enjoy life as vibrantly as she did, enjoying every moment. I guess anything is possible, isn't it?

And so it was that Rio entered my life, filled it with love, and turned it upside down very quickly. Life is not what it used to be, and will never be the same, and I am so much the better for it. Since I met Rio, I have tried many new activities, gone to so many new places, made wonderful new friends, and wrote this book to honor Rio and my dear family. In this process, I have gained back my excitement for life, learned much about who I am, my emotions, needs, and desires … and who I want to become in the future and what I need in my life to get there. I've also discovered the kinds of things I can no longer tolerate in my life. Because of this, I believe more really good things to come are on the horizon.

Rio and I communicate better every day. I believe this has come about because we enjoy doing so many things together and trying new activities that require us to be in sync with each other. Dog show training was the first step, where we learned to work as a team to be successful.

I think Rio has been able to learn so much because I make training fun and he always feels loved. That seems to increase his confidence, curiosity, and eagerness to go out and learn something new. I admire people who have had their own dogs since they were young and started showing them at a young age. I wish I was so lucky to have had my own show dogs when I was younger. But there are no regrets, I am so happy that Rio and I have each other now and try to enjoy every moment.

Unfortunately, dogs usually do not live as long as us. I found a great explanation for that on the Internet, by a six-year-old boy whose beloved dog had passed away:

> "People are born so they can learn how to live a good life — like loving everybody all the time, and being nice, right? Well, dogs already know how to do that, so they do not have to stay as long."
> Garry McDaniel, Author
> *The Dog's Guide to Your Happiness: Seven Secrets for a Better Life from Man's Best Friend.*

So true. Dogs already have it all together!

∞

After Pat's death, I felt inspired to write a book about her. That inspiration grew over time, and merged with my growing desire to honor Mom and Rio. Pat's life was cut short way too soon, and knowing Rio's life (any dog's life) is also way too short, has inspired me to begin writing a book now, while we are together, rather than putting it off.

Perhaps writing this book will be my way of keeping Rio, Pat, Mom, and my other family members' memories alive forever, to capture their love on paper and electronic pages before I pass and the memories of us fade.

Rio, a quick study, has been my guide and motivation every day while writing this book. It may seem funny that my inspiration has turned out to be an angel with fur, but Rio takes this job very seriously. He is by my side every day while I am writing, whether sleeping next to me so I can focus on the book, or staring at me and pawing me when he thinks it is time to take a break and give him some attention. When we are not working on the book, Rio is busy with training or fun antics, providing me with more subject material for the book!

We are so lucky to be together; I plan to enjoy every day with Rio! Who would not want to spend every day with someone who is very cute, fun, and loves them unconditionally?

I often speak words of love to Rio (sometimes to the jealousy of Joe).

Why? Because Rio is my heart and soul. He showers me with kisses every day. He makes me complete. As Emily Bronte wrote in Wuthering Heights, "Whatever our souls are made of, his and mine are the same." That is us.

He has given me courage and purpose again when nothing else seemed right, when no one else could get me out of my slump. He gave me my self-esteem back. I believe Rio actually saved my life … by giving me a new life.

He makes me laugh, smile, and do silly things, and do things I normally would not have the courage or confidence to do, such as enter Westminster. I feel I can do most anything I set my mind to with Rio by my side. I have driven for hours to strange places just to run around a ring with him for three minutes in front of hundreds of people we do not know. I drove for three hours through that snow storm just to NQ (my fault), but it was worth it just being with him. Other times we drove three hours and won a major in the conformation ring.

It has been worth traveling so far to sometimes win some nice ribbons and titles. Rio has made me feel like I am on top of the world, sometimes over the moon. He is my very first show dog, and I sure hope he is not my last!

Rio is a true angel, who has made so many people very happy, at the nursing homes and hospice and various hospitals. He makes my heart very proud of him.

He gives me goals and keeps me busy every spare moment. I joke that my planning calendar is no longer mine, though I still use it for my personal commitments. It is called "Rio's Calendar." Rio inspires me to get up and do things at really crazy-early hours. He is there by my bed next to me every morning when I make the smallest movement or turn over. If I sleep too long, he seems to know when the alarm is supposed to go off and stands next to me, staring.

If I do not open my eyes as soon as he approaches, he nudges me persistently with his nose until I awake. Next, he gives me his famous Rio stare, "Are you ready for a walk, Mum? Are you ready? Can we go to training, or to a show now, or to the nursing home? Where are we going today, Mum?"

He then follows me into the bathroom. I start to get dressed, with him hanging on every word I say. Most mornings I then go with Rio and Romeo for our early morning walk. Without Rio and our daily activities, I would be much more voluptuous than I am. He makes me get up to go out no matter what time it is or how tired I am.

He is my guide and has taken me to new places, encouraged me to meet new people and to participate in new activities, such as our work as a therapy dog team and different dog sports. He was the inspiration for writing this book and learning social media, something I pledged I would never do. Rio has also motivated me to start work on writing another love story.

He loves me unconditionally, and there are no games between us except fun ones. There are no lies, no deception, and no intentionally hurting me, unlike so many of the human relationships I have experienced. All Rio wants is to be with me and to enjoy every day to the fullest. As many people have said, if people were like dogs and had the values that dogs do, the world would be a much better place.

Rio has taught me to slow down and relax and to enjoy every moment, content to lie by my side for hours and get belly rubs. He has taught me to just sit on the couch for an hour and simply enjoy having his paw on my arm as I stare into his lovely almond-shaped eyes.

He has helped me to smell the roses again, by teaching me to go for long walks simply because we still can, and to stop and watch the leaves fall, or the birds land, and the squirrels run behind a tree, or just to have some time together. We have had fun spending many minutes at the storm sewer runoffs, where he thought he smelled a groundhog or some other animal, maybe a rat from Barn Hunt.

Everything seems good when Rio is by my side. I live in the moment and do not care about the time or the weather; nothing else matters because we are together. We often just do our spins and leg weaves and dance and have a grand laugh together!

Just to be with Rio makes me feel happy, he has shown me what pure, honest love is all about. I love Rio and what he is. It does not matter where we are, we are together and we are content with each other. We are complete. That is how I feel.

CHAPTER 53

The Time Of My Life

"The best time of my life has been loving you and being with you."

—Joni

I came across a couple of short articles years ago that I hold dear to my heart. They apply to so many dear people who have crossed my path in some way.

The first said that blessed beings, some call them angels, come down from heaven (or from your favorite sacred place) in various forms, and cross our paths at some time in our life. Some come to love us, help us, or teach us something. Some come in the form of family, friends, and neighbors. Others are co-workers, instructors, or a smiling stranger we meet on the street. Some are people on social media that we may never meet in person, but who have had the most profound impact on our lives and have motivated us greatly to come alive again, to love intensely, and be the person we always dreamed of ... and to always desire more from life, every moment of life.

Some stay with us for a long time, perhaps being here before we arrive and leaving before we do, like our parents. Others come for only a moment, to help us in a time of need, perhaps to motivate us, teach us something important, open a door when our hands are full, or to say hello to us as we enter the elevator, making us feel momentarily cheerful when we are having a stressful or daunting day.

I read somewhere that this is called the "conveyor of life."

Some of our blessed beings or angels get on the conveyor of our lives before we do, and some after. We all stay for different lengths of time, and leave at different times. It becomes part of the mysterious journey of life.

On my conveyor of life, I think of the angels who have meant the most to me, including those who have loved me, taken care of me, and taught me important things along the way. I fondly remember those who have been kind to me for a few moments, but whose kindness made such a strong impact on my life that I will never forget them.

Some of the angels have been people I have never met but who did kind acts, such as those very kind people who spent many of their days helping find Romeo, a dog they never met. And there are many other angels I do not know who have helped me in unknown ways as our paths crossed for a short time. For all of you, I am grateful.

My angels have come in all forms too — human, such as my family, my dear Mom, Dad, Pat, William, and other family, my friends, and kind strangers. And then there's the non-human angels in nature. So many other beings and forces have crossed my path and lifted my spirits time and time again — the sun on my face, the cheerful birds singing on a spring day, a fawn who wanted to play with me like a puppy, the bat who skimmed the water right next to me in a swimming pool, a colorful butterfly, sweet ladybug, or busy bee and dragonfly landing on me.

I have no doubt that angels also come with fur, as did Rio, my personal angel with fur, and my other dogs, Romeo, Marly, Shaman, Shaolin, Bijou, and all I have been lucky to share my life with. Rio, my darling boy, my funny Valentine, my leprechaun, my charming munchkin who makes me laugh, the big-hearted dog who puts his paw on me while getting his belly rubbed and then kisses me. The handsome, flirtatious gentleman who stops suddenly while we are on a walk and waits for me to catch up to him, then flips his head up to give me a kiss.

Rio is my best furry friend who leads me to so many fun places. He is the beguiling darling who invites me to dance with him when I least expect it, but probably most need it, the compassionate furry man who does a trick for the people at the nursing home, then turns to them, smiles and licks their hand.

I thank you, Rio, for coming my way and being in my life.

Rio means "river" in many languages. Rio truly is my river, a giver of renewed life to me and the provider of many of my most memorable exciting journeys. I thank you for giving me my life back and giving me my desire to live again, and goals and ambitions to do things once more.

∞

Rio just turned 10 years old. It is sad seeing him grow old. Where has all that time gone so quickly? Looking back to when he was a pup, there is a difference in energy. Rio has slowed down a bit. He tires more easily and sleeps more, and has gotten greyer on his eyebrows and muzzle. He is in the prime of his life, or maybe he is in the autumn of his life, as Frank Sinatra sang.

Like a good wine improving with age, Rio is more physically beautiful than ever, with his coat so plush and thick. He still has lots of energy and alertness, so much that people believe he is much younger than he is. As Rio has matured gracefully, his personality has rounded out nicely, being more confident and outgoing with those we meet. He has lots of love in him, and I feel it more every day. Our relationship has become even closer as time has gone on. We are soul mates, and we seem to think alike and read each other's minds at times.

So where do we go from here? I do not know what the future will bring, other than that one day, way too soon, Rio will pass over the Rainbow Bridge. I do believe he will look deep into my eyes as he leaves me, to say, "Mum, what are you ever going to do without me by your side? What will you do until we meet again at the Rainbow Bridge? You know I love you, and I will miss you greatly every day until then Mum...."

Yes, I will miss him greatly. When Rio passes, it will be the end of a great era and the best time of my life.

Until then, I will do all I can to take good care of him and keep him healthy and very happy as we keep busy and do all that we can together. We will visit the nursing homes and hospice to cheer up people, we will go on long rides to dog trials and training, to the Jersey shore and nearby parks to walk and do Parkour, and for long walks looking for squirrels and storm water drains for fun.

We will play together, we will dance and do spins and leg weaves and smile and laugh, and I will give him his favorite belly rubs, body scratches, and paw rubs every day. He is my best buddy, and he deserves all these good things and all things good, and more.

As someone Unknown said about a dog:

"He is your friend, your partner, your defender, your dog. You are his life, his love, his leader. He will be yours, faithful and true, to the last beat of his heart. You owe it to him to be worthy of such devotion."

Yes, that is Rio, and I will try to be the person he thinks I am until I cannot anymore.

I will always love my Rio and take the best care of him I can. I am so proud of you, Rio, and I will always love you to infinity and back. I love you more than I love myself, and I will love you for eternity, my darling, my Rio.

Oops! I have to go now. Work is closed today because of the nor'easter that is expected to arrive in a few hours. I bet Pat sent this blizzard as a gift to me, a much-needed snow day, knowing I would think of her and miss her tremendously.

Rio knows this, and just came over to tell me to get off the computer. He is standing next to me and staring at me with those sweet, soft, almond-shaped brown eyes as he paws my arm gently.

"It's time to do something with *me* now, Mum! Let's go outside and go for a walk before the storm gets here! Hurry, Mum! Let's go!"

10 years old, Rio. I hope you can stay a long time yet. This has truly been the time of my life.

"We were together, and I forgot the rest"

—*Walt Whitman*

References

American Temperament Test Society, Inc., Temperament Evaluation Regulations, Retrieved 18 March, 2019 from https://atts.org/wp-content/uploads/2017/03/ATTS_TER.pdf

Cambridge Dictionary > Zany, Retrieved March 21, 2019 from https://dictionary.cambridge.org/dictionary/english/zany

Dog Scouts of America > Our Mission, Retrieved March 14, 2019 from http://dogscouts.org/base/?fbclid=IwAR0SFRaihrGDeNNg3j1iJFVgfLXrcN4IpX2MUuw4Fx5-0IZ0rlGY_c45mIA

Goodreads, Emily Bronte > Quotes, Retrieved March 14, 2019 from https://www.goodreads.com/author/quotes/4191.Emily_Bront_

McDaniel, Garry. 2017. The Dog's Guide to Your Happiness: Seven Secrets for a Better Life from Man's Best Friend. Metuchen, New Jersey: CompanionHouse Books.

Pet Partners > Home > About, Retrieved 18 March, 2019 from https://petpartners.org/

About the Author

*J*oni lives in the beautiful mountains of New Jersey on the East Coast of the United States, works to save our Earth's environment and biodiversity and loves life with Rio and Romeo.

Please tweet a photo of you and your
dog or other pet with Rio's book to share
with us on Twitter at @arc_shepherd.
Rio and I would love to see a photo of you!

CPSIA information can be obtained
at www.ICGtesting.com
Printed in the USA
BVHW092128261119
564890BV00002B/4/P